Portraits of Creative Aging

Portraits of Creative Aging
Living Longer and Better

Joan Kadri Zald

PORTRAITS OF CREATIVE AGING

10 9 8 7 6 5 4 3 2 1

ISBN 978-0-9827846-0-0

Published by
CORBY BOOKS
A Division of Corby Publishing LP
P.O. Box 93
Notre Dame, Indiana 46556
(574) 784-3482
www.corbypublishing.com

MANUFACTURED IN THE UNITED STATES OF AMERICA

To my husband, Mayer,
who has been on this journey with me

Contents

1

In Search of Role Models

*A*t age sixty-five, draftsman John Chan retired from the California Highway Department. Fulfilling a long-term dream, which had been denied because of poverty and life circumstances, Mr. Chan at age seventy-six, received a Bachelor of Fine Arts Degree in Photography from the Academy of Art College in San Francisco. His work brought him such notice that he was recognized as a Fellow at the Royal Photography Society of Great Britain. At age eighty-nine, he was still learning and experimenting with new photographic techniques. Mr. Chan has had fifteen solo exhibits, including shows in China and England.

After serving forty years as an elementary school teacher, Doris Sperling, now in her seventies, was so concerned about the achievement gap between white and black students that she spearheaded the founding of the Family Learning Institute in Ann Arbor, Michigan. Under her leadership, the Institute's one hundred fifteen volunteers have bolstered opportunities for numerous low-income, low-achieving students by providing free tutoring.

1

Kenneth Lajoie worked for thirty years as a geologist at the United States Geological Survey. In his sixties and retired from the Survey, he is now doing something to which he always aspired—participating in archeological digs. His expertise in geology opened the door for him to work at ancient Egyptian sites as both a geologist and amateur archeologist. He is thrilled to explore the ancient villages thought to have housed the builders of the famous pyramids of Giza.

After the showing of a film in Nashville, Tennessee, graphically documenting the pollution, raw sewage and trash in the Cumberland River, Shirley Caldwell Patterson felt something urgent needed to be done and spearheaded the founding of the Cumberland River Compact. The Compact, with the aid of water-quality professionals, educates, mentors and advises citizen committees in the fourteen watersheds of the river. This has led to remarkable river improvement. Ms. Patterson and the Compact have won numerous conservation awards as well as a grant from the Environmental Protection Agency. At the time she started the Compact, Shirley Caldwell Patterson was seventy-nine years old.

Lois Nochman has been swimming in Masters competitions for over seventeen years. A retired community college teacher, her competitive swimming career began at age sixty-four. She always loved to swim but team swimming had not been available to her in high school and college; Title IX, which promoted equal athletic opportunities for women, did not pass until 1972. In her eighties, she is still the envy of her opponents as she has won over 1000 medals and set thirty-five national records and thirty-eight world records.

How did they do it?
What did it take?

I needed to know. In my sixties, although I was very healthy and active, I experienced fleeting moments of dread and anxiety when I thought about turning seventy. In addition to a heightened awareness of my mortality, I feared that stagnation and decline lay just around the corner. I had less anxiety about how long I would live, as most family members of my parents' generation lived into their eighties and my maternal grandmother lived to age ninety-two. Much of my apprehension was about *how* I would live because of the examples my relatives had set. They had all withdrawn, to varying degrees, from involvement in life as they grew older. I did not want to follow that path.

I remember feeling much sadness when a favorite aunt, who had been lively, opinionated, and interested in the world around her, began to socially withdraw when she was in her late sixties or early seventies. She became increasingly preoccupied with her aches and pains, citing various physical complaints as the reason she continually turned down social invitations. She ceased to participate in the art activities she loved and appeared to lose her previously held intense interest in the activities and comings and goings of her friends and family. I recall actually feeling a sense of loss when she stopped peppering me with personal questions and giving me her usual unsolicited advice. As I look back, even though my relatives lived long lives, not one of them provided me with a good model of aging. In retrospect, I am sure some of this was due to their struggles with illness and disability, not unusual in those days.

As a way of coping with my irrational fear that all the activities and projects I loved would suddenly grind to a halt on that feared day when I turned seventy, I started searching for positive role models of aging. I was especially interested in people in their sixties, seventies and eighties who were leading active, creative and productive lives. It turned out that

I already knew some and I was able to see them with "new eyes" once I started looking. Along the way, I found other older people like John, Doris, Ken, Shirley and Lois, who were doing amazing things.

Doris was one of the people I encountered, quite serendipitously, when the idea for this project was just beginning to gel. My daughter, then a teenager, had been a member of Young Peoples Theater, a drama group Doris had founded, and I had met Doris back in those long ago days. We renewed our acquaintance when, prior to a presidential election, I was manning a voter registration booth in a small shopping center where Doris' Family Learning Institute was located. She invited me on a tour of her facility once my shift ended. She clearly was very proud of the Institute and wanted me to know about the work they were doing and the positive results they were achieving. I was struck by her warm and relaxed manner with the children as well as her enthusiasm when discussing her plans for the Institute. I came away feeling deeply moved, and for many days after kept thinking about the passion, drive and accomplishment of this seventy-three-year-old woman. She gave me a sense of what was possible.

As I located more and more people in this search and observed the quality of their lives, I realized how many of my attitudes about aging were inaccurate and dated. The people I found were engaged in life and they were continuing to grow and develop. Their creativity, *the process of bringing something new into being—an idea, an activity or a product,* and their productivity, *the creation of goods and services of value,* enriched their lives and the lives of people in their communities. I felt inspired by these encounters and I began to assemble a collection of photographs and narratives, based on interviews with these creative and productive people.

I am a retired social worker and photographer (I started studying photography when I was fifty) and I often combine both sets of skills and interests to explore social issues and problems. Reflecting this synthesis, in one earlier undertaking I documented the plight of homeless men and women through stories and photographs. So the notion of taking pictures, as well as conducting in-depth interviews, seemed natural to me.

Friends and family found the stories I was gathering personally empowering and this led me to consider bringing them together in a book. I then proceeded to expand my search in order to have an ample collection of different role models. I tried to make the pool of participants diverse by interviewing people with a variety of skills, from distinct geographic regions and from different ethnic and racial backgrounds.

As a former social worker, I thought these stories would also be helpful to professionals who work with an older population, as they show the importance of creative and productive activities in enhancing the quality of life and well being of older adults. In addition, many of the stories illustrate the benefits to human service organizations and communities when older citizens have the opportunity to put their talents and experience to good use.

As the number of interviews grew, I was able to identify the pertinent characteristics and behaviors that these creative older people had in common. This enabled me to develop guidelines and strategies to help others and myself, in the process of creative aging. How did they do it? What did it take? My findings and ensuing suggestions later in the book are addressed to people who are contemplating or preparing for retirement or have recently retired, and to professionals who work with people of traditional retirement age. I hope the stories are a source of inspiration to all readers.

Albine Bech* has been an inspiration and role model to many people who know her. As a teenager in France, her ambition to become a physical education teacher was denied because of the advent of the Second World War. Now retired and on the cusp of turning eighty, she teaches Tai Chi and Water Aerobics, tutors elementary school students and has taught other older people how to use the Web-TV technology. She has finally realized her dream of becoming a teacher.

*Chapter 3

Today's Older Population
("Down-aging"—Eighty the New Sixty?)

Although I had a long career as a clinical social worker, I had limited experience working with an older population and minimal interest in gerontology. To make up for these deficits, I started reading the current literature on aging. A number of books and research reports enabled me to be a more "tuned in" interviewer and helped me understand more about aging in America today. Books by Gene D. Cohen,[1] Marc Freedman[2] and John W. Rowe and Robert L. Kahn[3] were especially helpful as were some U.S. Census Bureau reports[4] and news releases.[5]

Dramatic changes have occurred in the health and longevity of the older population in this country. Older Americans today are markedly different than the elderly of previous generations. They are living longer, healthier lives with far fewer disabilities; they are better educated than ever before; have better financial resources; and are less likely to be poor compared to prior generations.

People today live thirty years longer than they did a century ago. The average life expectancy in 1900 was forty-seven, it is now close to seventy-nine and rising. An American reaching sixty-five today has a life expectancy of an additional eighteen years and a twenty-five percent likelihood of reaching age ninety. Older Americans now compose a larger segment of the population than ever before. There are now thirty-five million Americans over age sixty-five and the number of older Americans is expected to significantly increase as the seventy-eight million baby boomers (those born between 1946 and 1964) grow older. The U.S. Census Bureau estimates that there will be seventy million Americans age sixty-five and over (twenty percent of the population) in 2030.

It is predicted that individuals who have recently retired, or will soon retire, may live in relatively good health for a number of decades after their work years. The health of older Americans keeps improving. This is a result of advances in science, medicine, sanitation, as well as life changes made by a better educated and informed population. Older Americans today when compared to older Americans twenty years ago, show substantially less disability. While many will eventually become disabled, it will occur much later in life—scientists refer to this as an increase in health expectancy. Although there are older Americans who live with severe disabilities and/or financial hardship, the percentages have significantly declined.

These changes in health and longevity have led to a revised view of aging along with the introduction and use of new terms such as "prime time" and "down-aging." An article in *Parade* magazine[6] reported on the results of a survey in which readers were asked for the names they preferred to describe the twenty year span between sixty and eighty. Among the four thousand respondents, the vast majority of those over sixty rejected "senior citizen," and chose "prime time" as their favorite term. "Down-aging," an increasingly popular term, highlights the advances that have occurred in the health and functioning of the older population and is employed to describe older people who are comparable in health and vigor to younger people of an earlier time. For instance, eighty year olds are seen as being comparable to sixty year olds of the previous generation.

In keeping with the "prime time" perspective, an additional life stage or period reflecting the changing demographics has been added to models of the life course by a number of writers. This life stage, often called "The Third Age,"[7] is defined as the period between adulthood and true old age. Referring to the years between fifty or sixty and eighty, it is seen as a time of prolonged health and newfound freedom, offering possibilities of growth and development and a chance to pursue new and different endeavors. Some writers may differ slightly about the age parameters and tasks of the third age, but the general concept is the same.

Along with this shifting perspective, gerontologists have begun to use the term "oldest-old" for those over eighty or eighty-five. This group is the fastest growing segment among the older population. This late-life stage is seen as one of decreasing activity and functioning and increasing health concerns. Still, there is great variation in the aging process and the number of people in this age group who continue to be active and high functioning is on the rise. Among them are the people over eighty presented in this book.

The third age concept is well represented by Berdelle Campbell.* She and her husband, grandparents to seven grandchildren, are approaching their eightieth year. A self-described full-time community volunteer since her retirement, Berdelle's life is a whirlwind of activity. Her community advocacy activities have included working to revitalize a decaying inner-city neighborhood, historic restoration, promoting recycling programs, protecting air and water quality, encouraging citizen participation via work for the League of Women Voters and supporting programs for disadvantaged children. She feels a deep commitment to improving her community for the welfare of all citizens, and says she would be denying herself if she didn't participate, as she receives so much satisfaction out of what she does.

*Chapter 4

Caught in a Lag
(And Why We Need Role Models)

At the same time that there is a growing recognition of the demographic changes in our society, the behaviors and attitudes of a portion of the public do not reflect awareness or acknowledgement of these advances. A director of research at the National Institute of Aging, Richard Suzman, Ph.D., referred to this discrepancy in a 2006 news release.[8] He commented that despite the substantial changes that have occurred over the past two decades, many people still maintain an image of aging that is twenty years out of date. Twenty years out of date!

Sociologists see this outdated image, to which Dr. Suzman refers, as a component of the "structural lag."[9] Matilda White Riley, a sociologist and gerontologist, developed the concept to describe the lack of adaptation in the latter part of the twentieth century to the rapidly changing gains in health and longevity of older Americans. She and her colleagues saw the lag as being due to the entrenched and slow-changing nature of national policies and institutions. As a result, roles and opportunities were out of step with the interests and capacities of older citizens. Dr. Riley and her colleagues observed that the sluggish pace of change was discernable not only in institutions but also in the attitudes, many of them negative, about aging and older people. We still see aspects of this lag today in the twenty-first century, as a number of attitudes, public policies and practices have not adjusted. More appropriate roles and norms of aging have not replaced the old, outmoded ones.

Negative stereotypes still abound and continue to exact a toll, as does "elderspeak," belittling, disrespectful and infantilizing forms of address (sweety, deary). Recent studies[10] have found that levels of functioning and health can be adversely affected when older individuals accept the negative stereotypes of aging. Difficulty in resisting the stereotypes can cause people to walk more slowly, hear and remember less and even affect their cardiovascular systems. Conversely, individuals with positive attitudes about aging stay healthier longer.

The structural lag certainly contributed to my own mind-set about aging. I realize now that my earlier fears were due not only to the lack of good models of aging in my family but also to the outdated image of older people, along with the negative stereotypes, which persist in our society. Awareness of older people who carve out new paths for themselves can help change these dated perceptions and deleterious attitudes. These role models offer inspiration, a sense of possibilities, options and direction. In addition, on a societal level, they can aid in the expansion of opportunities, as they demonstrate how older citizens can, and do, continue to contribute to society.

Henry Foster Jr.,* provides us with an example of someone who has fashioned new roles for himself. Seven years ago, he officially retired from Meharry Medical College, where he had served in many positions, including Chair of the Department of Obstetrics and Gynecology. Throughout his illustrious career, he worked tirelessly to improve the maternal and infant care of poor patient populations as well as provide first-class medical training to *students and residents. Now age seventy-three, he has continued his work in new and different ways. He is on three medical school trustee boards and is presently Chairman of the Board of Directors of Pathfinder International, a non-profit organization devoted to providing family planning and reproductive health services in the developing world.*

*Chapter 2

Role Models Found

Social contacts and networks played an essential role in my search. Since I wanted to include people from a number of different geographic regions of the country beyond my home base in Southeastern Michigan, I chose places where I had previously lived (Nashville, Tennessee, and the San Francisco Bay area) or where I knew people (Los Angeles, Tucson, and New York City). I proceeded to enlist the assistance of friends, acquaintances and family members in those cities, and asked them to mine their social networks for me. The search had been relatively easy in and around Ann Arbor, Michigan, where I have lived much of my adult life. It initially proved more difficult in the other communities where I had fewer contacts and networks. I began to realize that in contrast to famous older people, like Mike Wallace or Clint Eastwood, the people I sought were often under the radar.

When I first started asking for assistance in my search, people seemed unaware that the type of person I sought existed. In some cases they actually knew them, but didn't really "see" them, similar to my own experience at an earlier time. My hunch is that this is a by-product of the structural lag—we tend not to expect, and therefore don't see or recognize, the vibrant, creative older people around us. On the other hand, we do expect, and consequently do see, those who present the negative face of aging. I began to hit pay dirt in my search when I made contact with some "creative agers," as they often had circles of friends and acquaintances similar to themselves. This sometimes created a snowball effect and I ended up interviewing more people than I was able to include in the book.

There were times when finding particular interviewees involved three to four "degrees of separation," necessitating a chain of referrals, one contact leading to another, until I found the type of person I sought. No one I asked turned down my request for an interview. Two or three women initially expressed qualms about having their pictures taken but all eventually consented.

Locating and making contact with the participants who lived far from my home, as well as traveling to meet them, was the most difficult and fatiguing part of the process. But it always turned out to be well worth the effort. Not only did I learn about the present-day activities of those I interviewed, I frequently heard their life stories, which invariably were fascinating. They exposed me to worlds and experiences far different from my own.

In listening to the stories, I often became privy to the hardships, losses and tragedies many had endured and survived. I received vivid glimpses of the difficulties of the immigrant experience and life under segregation. The Second World War had left its imprint on many. One woman was a Holocaust survivor, one man had suffered confinement in a Japanese-American internment camp, a few had lived through the occupation and deprivations of war in Western Europe, some men had served in the Armed Services during the war, and one had participated in the Normandy Invasion.

During some of the interviews, I felt that I was having the privilege of a private showing with an artist. This was true when painters Fay Kleinman and Sheldon Markel showed me works in progress in their studios, when photographer John Chan retrieved his wonderful photographs from storage boxes and cabinets, and when Gene Schklair took me on a tour of his sculpture and explained the messages he hoped they conveyed. Sometimes the interviews turned into fun, as when Ken Lajoie and I compared notes about the ancient cities and archeological sites we had visited, and our lists of sites we still hoped to visit some day. I always came away from interviews energized and excited, almost bursting with the need to tell someone, usually my husband, who became equally excited.

Very often, the interviewees and I established a strong connection or bond as they shared their stories with me. It was not unusual for an interview to end in hugs. Many of the interviewees still keep in contact with me and send me up-to-date information on their activities. I've wondered, why have I felt such a strong connection to the people I interviewed? After all, in my work as a social worker I listened to people's stories, their traumas, travails and triumphs, all the time. I think the difference is that I felt, with almost every interview, that I was on the receiving end and was being given a gift. Each person, openly and generously, provided me with an example of how it was possible to live creatively as one grows older.

In addition to seeking people from a number of geographic areas, I wanted people of different races and ethnicities represented, as well as a relatively equal balance of men and women. As I mentioned earlier, I was interested in locating people engaged in a broad range of creative and productive activities requiring different skills. I thought such a range was important, as I wanted the reader to obtain a sufficient number of different and realistic role models. None of the individuals in the book are famous, although some have achieved prominence in their fields or have received recognition in their communities. Basically, I wanted these exceptional people, who are also very real people, to be ones from whom you and I can learn. They are people who are making the most of the gifts of time and opportunity, and are demonstrating that creative aging is an obtainable goal.

When he was age fifty-four, doctors told Gene Schklair,* a dentist, that his lungs were failing and he had just a year to live. With grit and tenacity, he and his wife, Glorya, decided to make the most of his "last" year and backpack around the world. Upon their return, the ensuing search for the allergen that was killing him, eventually led to a cure. With a new lease on life, Gene, now in his seventies, turned to a previous, but never sufficiently fulfilled passion—sculpture. He has been a full-time sculptor for the past twenty years. This self-taught artist has been delighting audiences with his whimsical, yet serious, life-size plaster sculptures, exhibiting them in galleries, juried shows and art fairs.

*Chapter 5

Paths Taken

I interviewed a total of forty-five people over a period of four years (2005-2009). They all had wonderful stories to tell and I learned much from every one of them. This book is comprised of thirty-seven of those stories with accompanying photographs. The largest number of participants is in the seventy to seventy-nine age range. The age distribution at the time they were interviewed is as follows: sixty to sixty-nine (6), seventy to seventy-nine (19), eighty to eighty-nine (8), and ninety to ninety-five (4).

The participants' activities (it would be more accurate in some cases to call them second or third careers) are varied and, with just a few exceptions, fall into two major categories—the arts and community service. The arts include: painting, sculpture, photography, acting, directing, woodworking, writing, storytelling, as well as musical composing, conducting and performing. Some of the community service activities include: consulting, tutoring, teaching, coaching, and mentoring, as well as founding, leading and fundraising for organizations dedicated to conservation, education, health, community restoration, citizen participation, and advocacy for the homeless and the mentally ill. A number of individuals combined community service with their artistic activities. In addition, a few of the participants pursued scholarly and athletic endeavors.

Four different paths to the creative activities became apparent to me in the course of the interviews. Gene D. Cohen, in his book *The Creative Age: Awakening Human Potential in the Second Half of Life*,[11] proposes three different categories or paths to creativity in older people. The paths I've identified are somewhat different than his but I am indebted to him as his framework helped me conceptualize the four paths I saw. They include:

1. Creativity that continues and grows in later life;
2. Career or work skills that are applied in new ways in retirement;
3. Avocations that flourish in retirement;
4. New Beginnings—creative ventures that start in the retirement years.

The first path, *creativity that continues and grows in later life*, includes individuals who are involved in the same creative endeavors throughout most of their lives and continue to grow and develop in those endeavors. Fay Kleinman, in chapter two, is a good example of such a person. She has been an artist all her adult life and now, in her nineties, she is still painting in original and fresh ways. She recently completed a set of paintings using a new abstract style employing bold colors.

Carleen McGinn, also in chapter two, provides an example of the second path, *career or work skills applied in new ways in retirement*. A retired clinical social worker, she combined her considerable expertise as a counselor with her religious faith to become a Stephen Minister (a care-giving, lay counseling ministry within Protestant denominations). Her clinical skills are now put to use, not only in her role as a Christian counselor, but also as a trainer, supervisor and consultant to other Stephen Ministers. For people in this category, the contributions they make are far more important to them than any payment they may, or may not, be receiving.

Increased free time and fewer responsibilities are important ingredients for the third path—*avocations that flourish in retirement*. This group includes those individuals who have had lifelong avocations as well as those whose avocations began in late mid-life. Laurie (Lawrence) Naiman, in chapter three, fits into the lifelong avocation group. He became interested in photography as a teenager and continued to do photographic work throughout his student days and his professional career as a physician, specializing in pediatric hematology. He began to make changes in the quality and nature of his photography prior to retirement, and retirement allowed him to nurture, solidify and expand on those changes.

Sheldon Markel, also in chapter three, provides an example of those whose avocation started in late mid-life. In his fifties, encouraged by his wife, he took his first drawing class. He got "hooked" and began studying art with different teachers over a period of years. Now retired, he has more time to devote to his artwork and it has become an important part of his life and a source of much gratification. His paintings are shown in juried exhibits and galleries.

The fourth path, *new beginnings*, includes all those who launched into new creative ventures after retirement. Some started immediately upon retirement; others, after varying periods of time. Carrie Raiford, in chapter five, a professional storyteller, fits into this fourth group. Soon after her retirement as a childcare worker, she took advantage of the opportunity to become a storyteller, fulfilling a lifelong desire to become a public speaker.

People are multifaceted and some didn't fit into just one path or group; they overlapped or straddled two, and occasionally three groups. The overlapping usually occurred between paths one and two and between three and four. For this reason I've combined *creativity that continues and grows in later life* with *career or work skills applied in new ways* in chapter two. *Avocations that flourish in retirement* and *new beginnings* were combined for the same reason. I've divided this larger, second group, *avocations that flourish* and *new beginnings,* into three chapters. Chapter three includes individuals in fine arts, crafts and performing arts as well as those with physical accomplishments. Chapter four contains the stories of people primarily involved in community service. Chapter five presents individuals in both the arts and in community service whose endeavors developed, or were enhanced, as a result of their participation in community programs for older citizens. Chapter six looks at some of the common characteristics and behaviors in the lives of these thirty-seven vibrant, older individuals. Their lives offer us guidelines and strategies on how to be engaged, creative and productive as we age. Following chapter six, I pose some questions and suggestions based on these guidelines to help readers on their own paths toward creative aging. Professionals may also find these questions and suggestions helpful when exploring options with their older clientele.

2

Creativity Continuing and Work Skills Applied in New Ways

The stories of people following the first two creative paths are presented in this chapter. The first path is composed of individuals who have been engaged in creative work throughout their adult life and continue to be creative as they age. The second path contains those who have found new ways to apply their career or work skills in retirement. As mentioned earlier, some seem to fit into, or straddle, both groups. Participants' endeavors include scholarly pursuits, writing, the arts, and community or public service.

My major focus in all the interviews was on the development and role of creative and productive activities in the lives of the participants. It became apparent to me that the type of activities people chose, and the paths taken to achieve them, could be more fully appreciated when seen in the context of the *whole* person and his or her history and life situation. Most stories in the book therefore include some personal history as well as information on physical health and fitness, cognitive functioning, social relations, and religion and spirituality. The ages listed for all the contributors in the book were their ages at the time they were interviewed.[1]

Robert L. Kahn's narrative is the last one in this chapter. He is a family friend and one of the people I was able to see with "new eyes." He is also the author, along with John W. Rowe, of the book, *Successful Aging.*[2] In addition to his personal story, Bob reports on research findings on the characteristics or features shared by those who continue to flourish or do well, as they grow older (age successfully). The characteristics, which he views as the components of successful aging, include low risk of disease and disease-related disabilities, high physical and cognitive functioning and active engagement in life. In chapter six, we will see the importance of these characteristics in the lives of the people featured in this book.

1. Shirley Caldwell Patterson
    Founder and President of the Cumberland River Compact
    Conservationist

2. Henry W. Foster, Jr., M.D.
    Chair of Board of Directors of Pathfinder International
    Author of *Make a Difference*
    Professor Emeritus
    Meharry Medical College

3. Ray Nelson
    Restorer of Classic Cars

4. Doris Sperling
    Co-Founder and Executive Director of
    the Family Learning Institute

5. Kenneth Lajoie
    Geologist and Amateur Archeologist for Egyptian
    Archeological Excavations

6. Marilynn Rosenthal
   Author of *9/11: Searching for My Son and His Killers*
   Professor Emerita of Sociology
   University of Michigan

7. Jai-Zhen Song
   Composer and Conductor

8. Carleen McGinn
   Stephen Minister

9. Fay Kleinman
   Artist

10. Robert L. Kahn
    Co-author of *Successful Aging*
    Professor Emeritus of Psychology and Public Health
    University of Michigan

Shirley Caldwell Patterson
Age 87
Founder and President of the
Cumberland River Compact, Conservationist

For two months in the summer of 1996, a man named Victor Scoggins swam the entire 697 miles of the Cumberland River, which flows through Tennessee and Kentucky. He did it to draw attention to the pollution, raw sewage and trash in the river; the boat accompanying him had a banner reading "Save the Cumberland." His journey, graphically documenting the condition of the river, was filmed with a handheld camera. Scoggins showed the videotape to conservation groups and other organizations. A friend and I discussed the film after it was shown in Nashville in 1997, and almost in concert we said, "What can we do?" We didn't know what we could do but we knew we had to do something. I was 79 years old at the time.

We got together 8-10 friends who we thought would be interested in addressing this problem. This, in turn, led to our first public meeting, at which 60 people showed up, even though it was a cold, snowy, January night. We all sat in a double circle and went round and round, and everyone had an opportunity to express their thoughts about the river and to make suggestions. We all agreed that the river was in trouble. This style of meeting, which I believe in, and continue to use, enables everyone to be heard and to feel that what he or she says carries equal weight.

Thirty-five people signed up after the meeting and we started to meet every third week to discuss plans. One of our first decisions was to apply for a 501(c) designation (tax-exempt status for charitable and non-profit organizations). This made it necessary to create an organizational struc-

21

ture, along with bylaws and a mission statement and we officially formed the Cumberland River Compact. I was chosen President though it is a term I don't like; I consider myself a Chairperson. The mission of the Compact is to enhance the water quality of the Cumberland River and its tributaries through education and by promoting cooperation among citizens, businesses and agencies in Kentucky and Tennessee.

I had been involved in conservation work for decades before we formed the Compact. Although I never received a salary, conservation work has been my career. The process that eventually led to my commitment goes back to my midlife crisis. I married when I got out of school, which is what one did. I raised two splendid children and when they grew up I asked myself, "What now?" I felt I had three choices; I could become a proper matron, I could become a first-class alcoholic or I could do something else. I chose the latter path. I was almost 50 years old at the time and I had never been away from home by myself.

The beginning of that path dates back to a party my husband and I attended. A group of friends at the gathering were discussing a work/study program connected to an archeological dig in Greece. It sounded intriguing and I asked my husband if he would like to go with me. He had absolutely no interest in it. I took the big step and went ahead and joined up on my own. My world expanded; I took courses in Archeology and Greek after the dig, and for two months every summer for seven years, I worked on an ancient Greek excavation site in the Upper Galilee in Israel.

I had become an independent person and my husband and I eventually obtained a divorce. One of the many things I did on my own was join the Sierra Club. I became a serious backpacker and met Lucius Burch, who was also a backpacker, and we became very close friends. He was an attorney who divided his life between advocating for unpopular causes and exploring the wilderness of the earth. I went backpacking and fly-fishing in the Wyoming wilderness with Lucius and a group of friends three months every summer for fifteen years. This led to my love of the wilderness and my dedication to conservation. My spirituality lies in caring for the natural world.

I helped establish the Tennessee Environmental Council; I was treasurer of the Council for 17 years and served as President for many years. In addition, I was a member of the original Board of Trustees of the Nature Conservancy in Tennessee, was on the Board of the Tennessee Conservation League and was a member of the original Environmental Action Fund, which lobbied for natural resource management and protection.

I was confident the Cumberland River Compact would succeed because great strides had already been made since the passage of the Federal Clean Water Act. Discharges from factory pipes had come under stringent control resulting in significant improvement in water quality. The problems we face today are caused by discharges or runoffs from construction sites, farms, yards, highways and parking lots that pollute rivers and streams.

The Compact's organization and programs have grown since we started over eight years ago. In our first year we had no staff and the steering committee and the board of directors did all the work. We now have a staff of seven people. One of the first things we did was create the Water Quality Advisory Committee, a group of water quality professionals, to provide us with technical expertise. The committee is made up of professionals from federal, state and local agencies as well as academics and private consultants. This is the first committee in which conservation people from Tennessee and Kentucky have met together. The group has been meeting monthly for eight years. They provide us with up-to-date scientific information and check that any information we put out is technically accurate.

Fourteen major watersheds (a watershed is an area that drains water, dirt and dissolved materials to a common point) make up the Cumberland River Basin. In the past seven years, the Compact has worked with communities in seven watersheds and plans to eventually work with all fourteen. We mentor and educate the communities in each watershed. We assist them in putting together a local organization and provide professional facilitators to help them discuss what they see as the river's problems and what they want to do about them. We do not tell them what to do. We provide the information they need and translate complicated scientific reports on pollutants and other water problems into language the average person can understand. We also bring in scientists who are experts in the problems the communities want to tackle. As a result, the communities have done remarkable things to improve the seven watersheds.

In 2005, the Compact started a new program called the Local Officials Curriculum (LOC). We present, free of charge, educational seminars and didactic programs to hundreds of local policy makers and elected officials across the Cumberland Basin. We bring in the country's leading authorities to present current information on water issues and policies to help officials make informed decisions.

The Compact's approach is not the only one in conservation, but it has enabled us to be successful. We are non-confrontational and non-adversarial and we work by networking, dialogue, and education. I'd like to see our model used on a broader scale so that informed citizens and politicians can develop policies and solutions on a range of environmental problems. This has been a full-time job for me and it is on my mind much of the time. I see the protection of the quantity and quality of water as crucial for the survival of the human race.

My second full-time job is chair of the Lucius Burch Center in Wyoming, which I helped found. The Center was created in memory of Lucius Burch, who died in 1996, and loved the Wyoming high country. The Center's programs are designed to promote understanding between people of diverse backgrounds by fostering an appreciation and love for the wilderness. Following Lucius' death, three of his friends and I decided to edit and publish a collection of his writings. The book is entitled *Lucius: Writings by Lucius Burch*. We had it printed by a high quality, print-on-demand publishing business in Nashville. We think it is a beautiful book.

In addition to my son and daughter, I have two granddaughters. I've been living by myself in my apartment and I'm now in the process of getting ready to move into an independent living facility for seniors. The move will free me from responsibilities for my apartment so I can devote more of my energy and time to both the Compact and the Burch Center. There is still so much to do. You could say that what I'm doing now is paying my dues.

Nashville, Tennessee

Author's Note: A friend, who is very active in the Cumberland River Compact, told me about Shirley and referred to her as an icon in the conservation community in Tennessee. When I contacted Shirley, she expressed some reservation about meeting with me and indicated she was willing only because my friend, whom she respected, had vouched for me. We scheduled an appointment for a Sunday morning at her apartment. Because of our phone conversation, I was a little concerned that she might be a very reluctant interviewee. Fortunately, that was not the case. She was gracious and hospitable and her reticence quickly faded after we started talking. I was impressed with her vigor and the time and energy she, at age eighty-seven, was still devoting to conservation work. Also impressive was her continuing mastery of scientific information acquired from reading and the frequent meetings and presentations she attends.

She has lived a fascinating and adventurous life and in listening to her story, I was struck by her account of how her midlife crisis had been such a turning point and had changed the trajectory of her life.

I discovered, as a result of searching the web, that Shirley has been the recipient of a number of awards, including the Z. Carter Patten Award for outstanding contributions to conservation in Tennessee and the James R. Compton River Achievement Award. She has been invited to the White House and the Museum of Natural History in D.C. to make presentations. Under her leadership, the Cumberland River Compact has received numerous state conservation awards, as well as a large grant from the Environmental Protection Agency.

Henry W. Foster, Jr., M.D.
Age 73
Chair of Board of Directors of Pathfinder International
Author of *Make a Difference*
Professor Emeritus and
Former Dean and Vice President
for Medical Services, Meharry Medical College

> *My story is one of racism transcended and medical care*
> *reconceived, of moving from the poverty of the Deep South*
> *to the hallowed halls of Congress, of successful interventions*
> *and some failures, of working with people who don't have*
> *the resources to help themselves.*
>
> From *Make a Difference* by Henry W. Foster, Jr.

I was born and raised in Pine Bluff, Arkansas and had the good fortune of having wonderful parents. They were both schoolteachers who were well-educated, decent people with the highest integrity. They imbued certain values in my sister and me; one was that we had an obligation to leave the world a better place than we found it. I saw a career in medicine as a way to do that. I've tried to be an excellent physician, surgeon and teacher. Another value they imparted was: treat people as you would like to be treated. These guiding principles haven't changed for me over time.

I officially retired from Meharry Medical College in 1998 at age sixty-six. I truthfully hadn't given much thought to retirement. I knew it was a necessary formality for the school but I didn't plan to change much of what I was doing. My health was, and still is, good and I have lots of energy. My wife, Sandy, has asked, "Why do you still keep working? Haven't you worked enough?" But I love what I am doing and I think I still have something to offer. My father used to say, "If you have a job you really love, you never have to work another day in your life."

Aside from being an Emeritus Professor at Meharry, I'm also a clinical professor at Vanderbilt University Medical School. I came to Meharry from Tuskegee in 1973 to be Chairman of the Department of Obstetrics and Gynecology and served in that capacity for seventeen years. I then became Dean and Vice President for Health Services for four years and was Acting President of the Medical College for one year.

In 1995, President Bill Clinton nominated me to be U.S. Surgeon General. The Senate Labor and Human Resources Committee sent forward a favorable recommendation for my confirmation. Although abortion is a constitutionally protected right, opponents of abortion didn't let my nomination come to the Senate floor and denied me an up-or-down vote. I had performed a small number of abortions and had been the "physician of record" for others. Opponents of a woman's right to choose filibustered the nomination and some made outrageous allegations against me. I struggled to control my outrage at the malicious attacks on my character and the kind of person I am. It was clear I was being used as a proxy in the abortion debate and politicians were using this as they looked toward the upcoming election. A majority of fifty-seven Senators supported my nomination but they were three votes short of the sixty needed to break a filibuster.

My wife marveled at the objectivity I developed about some of the Senators' behavior and the politics involved. I recall being able to use that type of objectivity in my medical school days. In the 1950s, the University of Arkansas Medical School was attempting integration and enrolled a few African-American students. I applied to the school and was accepted. I was the only African-American in my class and I had to contend with eating in a separate cafeteria, with drinking from a separate water fountain, with social isolation and the racism of classmates. My father's words were invaluable, as he had taught me that the system was faulty; I wasn't. I thought if I had been brought up the way they had been, I might think exactly as my classmates did.

I was disappointed when the Senate failed to bring my nomination to the floor but other opportunities opened up for me. My father's words were again true, "When one door closes, another one opens." President Clinton invited me to be his Senior Advisor on Teen Pregnancy and Youth Issues. I served in that capacity from January 1996 to December 2001. In addition, a representative from Simon and Schuster, the publishing company, approached me about writing a book. They were aware that the millions of people who saw me on TV saw someone who was trying to do positive things, and they saw politicians trying to beat me up. They thought people would want to know more about me. The book *Make a Difference,* published in 1997, gave me the opportunity to say the things I wanted to say. It took me thirteen months to write and it is both an autobiography *and* a commentary on health care in America.

In writing the book and looking back on my career, there were a number of things that stood out to me. Among them, in addition to all the babies I have delivered, and the large number of medical students and residents I have trained, are the Tuskegee and *I Have A Future* programs. Early in my career, I chose employment at Tuskegee University (formerly Tuskegee Institute) in order to work with poor, disadvantaged, rural, mainly black women. Their plight was terrible and the lack of maternal and child care resulted in massive health problems and high infant mortality. I was determined to improve their health care and worked to develop a comprehensive program during my eight years there. The program   involved community outreach, specialized services for high-risk patients and pre- and postnatal care for mothers and infants. The Tuskegee Program later became a model for regionalized peri-natal care for the entire country.

Between 1981 and 1986, as a Senior Program Consultant for the Robert Wood Johnson Foundation, I directed a program to consolidate health services for high-risk young people. That work helped me conceptualize and develop the *I Have a Future* program in the late 1980s in Nashville. *I Have a Future* was designed, in consultation with parents, teenagers and the community, to reduce teen pregnancy, in addition to addressing other serious problems facing inner-city youth. The program, initially set in two housing projects, works to raise participants' self-esteem, promotes abstinence from sex, and offers positive options to help teenagers stay in school and go on to college. It has been a very successful program and continues to this day. In 1991, President George H. Bush recognized it as one of the nation's "Thousand Points of Light."

Some things have changed for me since retirement. My income now comes from retirement funds rather than the University and I no longer have onerous administrative responsibilities. I still teach and lecture to medical students and continue to do some office gynecology. I can now be more selective about the things I do. In fact, I just accepted a new responsibility. The Robert Wood Johnson Foundation recently asked me to chair their National Committee on Information Technology for County and City Public Health Departments.

I'm on a number of Boards; I'm presently chairman of the Board of Directors of Pathfinder International and I'm on three Medical School Trustee Boards, two in this country and one in South Africa. I am committed to my work on these Medical School Boards. I believe that if you make the schools as good as they can be, it translates into creating better health care professionals, which translates into better health care delivery, which ultimately translates into better health care outcomes.

Of these various activities, Pathfinder consumes a disproportionate amount of my time—but I love the organization and the wonderful work it does. I was invited to join the Board eight years ago and I have now been Chair for a year and a half. The Board plays a role in advocacy, fundraising and policy setting. Pathfinder International is a unique organization devoted to providing access to quality family planning and reproductive health information and services in the developing world. We work to halt the spread of HIV/AIDS, to provide care to women suffering from unsafe abortions and to advocate for sound reproductive health policies. The organization provides care in twenty-seven countries on three continents and utilizes the services of indigenous workers, physicians, nurses and local NGO's (non-governmental organizations). The services we provide are of immense value—they change and save lives!

This is a good time in my life, the best stage in my life. I'm engaged in activities that are important, that make a difference, and that are very gratifying to me. I am again fortunate as I have a wonderful family and I am healthy. I had some hypertension, which is now under control, and I stay fit by working out daily on a treadmill and by playing golf. I now get to play more golf (my golf game has never been better), and I had my first hole in one!

Nashville, Tennessee

Henry Foster (b. 1933) and his wife St. Claire (Sandy) have been married forty-six years and have a daughter, a son and two granddaughters. Sandy was a supervising nurse in a surgical recovery unit prior to her retirement. "Hank" is a graduate of Morehouse College and the University of Arkansas Medical School. In addition to playing golf, he enjoys reading, film and travel. He and his wife have traveled all over the world together. At one time he owned, and piloted, his own plane.

Raymond Nelson
Age 80
Restorer of Classic Cars

Working on cars keeps me interested in life. I love knowing how machines operate and I love solving the puzzles and finding the solutions when machines aren't operating properly. Every morning I look forward to working on a car, figuring out why something doesn't work and how to fix it.

I grew up on a farm in northern Michigan and after high school I attended Wayne University (now Wayne State University) in Detroit. I grew tired of school after two semesters and my roommate encouraged me to take a job and make good money hauling and delivering coal. So I started delivering coal in Detroit and Grand Rapids. We had to maintain our own trucks and as I couldn't afford a mechanic, I had to learn to do it myself. I had no training and taught myself about engines and brakes and so on. I made a lot of mistakes; that's how you become an expert, by making a lot of mistakes. I had been a member of the Future Farmers of America in high school and their motto was *Learn to Do by Doing.* That became my motto as well.

A vision problem kept me out of World War II and for two years I worked at a war plant building diesel pumps at night, while I continued to haul coal during the day. The plant closed after the war and I went back to the farm for a time to decide what to do next. My brother and I visited an aunt in Beverly Hills in 1947 and that trip started me thinking about getting out of Michigan's cold climate and moving to California.

I made the move to Los Angeles a few years later with my first wife. I initially worked at a gas station and then got a job at a Lincoln-

33

Mercury dealership where they put me to work fixing engines. It was the first of many jobs I had repairing cars for dealerships. I was sent to the GM center in Burbank for training and specialized in electrical problems. That continues to be a good specialty as everyone has electrical problems with their cars: the car won't start, instruments don't work, lights and signals are funny, cruise control isn't functioning, etc. There are more and more electrical functions in new cars and so more things can go wrong. I worked for dealerships for a total of twenty-five years until the last dealership I worked for closed. I was fifty-nine at the time. I guess you could say I was semi-retired for six years after that. I did some work as a mechanic at a local gas station and I also worked as a smog inspector.

I always fixed my own cars, which were old, in order to keep them running. Sometime in 1966 I started thinking that since I worked on my own cars, why not buy other old cars and repair and sell them. It began as a type of hobby and I've been doing it ever since. I don't do it so much for the money but because I love doing it. As soon as people find out that I have this skill or talent they contact me about an old car to buy. It's all been by word of mouth. The circle of acquaintances that send me cars keeps expanding. I sell the cars I've repaired by advertising in used car publications.

I work mostly on American cars; a car must be a certain make, with a certain problem and I must have the tools to fix it. I can't fix everything. GM cars have been my specialty for all these years. I became interested in MOPAR cars (the umbrella name for Chrysler products) when I bought a Chrysler wagon I wanted to use for camping. I rebuilt the engine of the wagon and I was able to drive it over the Rockies. I found it to be a very interesting car. Someone found out that I was interested in MOPAR cars and guess what? They had a used car for me.

My first wife and I divorced in 1969 after eighteen years of marriage. I married my second wife, Joanne, in 1980. In 1986, I won $25,000 in the lottery and that gave me a cushion, which enabled me to totally retire and graduate to my back yard (which is where I work on cars). I was getting bored with smog control and Joanne encouraged me to stop working. She and I are both low-upkeep people and don't need lots of money.

Retirement made it possible for me to work on complete classic car restorations. A cosmetic restoration just makes a car look good and a mechanical restoration gets it running well. A complete restoration does both and takes an enormous amount of time. The average time for me to do one is nine to ten months. I'd have to look up my records to see how many I've done but I'd say at least a dozen.

In 1993, when Columbia Pictures was planning a sequel to *My Girl*, they were looking for a suitable old truck to use as the featured car. My Corvair Rampside pickup was ready and they picked my truck over some others that applied. I had completed the restoration the year before and it was beautiful. Unfortunately, the director thought it was too "bright" and it was painted and lettered over, which made it look quite rough. Still, a collector in New York bought it as a movie car.

I've been working for five years on the Desoto that is presently in my garage. That's the longest I've ever worked on a car. Every bolt, every panel, every piece of the car has had my attention. The car is now drivable but I can never completely finish the cosmetic restoration because many of the materials are no longer available.

In addition to cars, I recently became interested in computers. I have a friend who builds computers and he has been teaching me. Working on computers, like working on cars, involves figuring out how things operate.

I'll soon be eighty-one and I've been in good health. All my physical problems have been due to accidents, like burns and cuts. I keep fit and get a good workout by going square dancing three times a week. I've been square dancing for fifty years.

Santa Monica, California

———————

Raymond Nelson (b. 1925) and his wife, Joanne, have been married for twenty-five years. Ray and his first wife had four daughters and Joanne had three children from her first marriage. Both Ray and Joanne experienced the tragedy of losing a child. Joanne's youngest son died in 1994 and one of Ray's daughters died in a car accident the following year. Ray has four grandchildren and Joanne has one granddaughter. In addition to cars and computers, Ray's past and present interests include mountain climbing, camping, fixing cameras, photography and processing black and white film in the chemical darkroom.

Doris Sperling
Age 74
Co-Founder and Executive Director of
the Family Learning Institute

I taught for forty years and I loved being a classroom teacher, but I really think the Family Learning Institute is the best thing I've ever done. We are taking children destined for a life of failure and turning their lives around.

I retired from elementary school teaching at age 63 in 1994 although I stayed in education by working for the North Central Association, a national accrediting and professional development organization. I also started tutoring two boys the summer I retired. Though they were in the fourth grade, they couldn't read, and I had to start from scratch. I worked with them in their homes, weekly for five years. Much of what I learned from tutoring them I put to use at the Family Learning Institute.

In my thirty-five years with the Ann Arbor Public Schools, I was continually concerned about the achievement gap between white and black students and once I retired I wanted to do something to address that gap. I brought together a group of people interested in the problem and in 1996 we formed the Community Academic Success Team (CAST). One of the first things we did was hold a town meeting and invite the community to come and tell us their opinions about the achievement gap. I also invited the school superintendent and school board members. As I knew these people so well, I could direct them that they couldn't talk, they just had to listen. The first town meeting at a black church was very successful. We attracted additional people who were interested in working on the problem. We held subsequent town meetings and wrote two position papers.

One night, five of us got together at my house to discuss what to do next. We talked about different strategies but we were really feeling discouraged about whether or not we would be able to bring about change. One of the members, Lefiest Galimore, a community services professional who later served as one of our Executive Directors, said, "Why don't we just do it ourselves?" There was dead silence. I thought about it overnight and called him the next morning and said okay. The issue was too dear to my heart to give up on it. So we did it ourselves!

We committed ourselves to plan, design and implement what became the Family Learning Institute. The program we now have was based on the recommendations of five focus groups, representing diverse segments of the community, in addition to our own thinking. We decided to target students in grades four through eight who were reading below grade level and were from low-income families. In the program, each student attends a free-of-charge, two-hour session once a week in the late afternoon or evening. During that time they receive help with reading, writing, thinking and questioning skills. The children are expected to attend regularly as well as read at home for thirty minutes a day, five days a week. Parents are expected to ensure their children's attendance and are assisted in developing skills to help their children become better learners.

We first opened our doors in March 2000, and started with two students. The next week we had eight students and now we are up to one hundred fifteen students and are open four days a week. The Ann Arbor Public Schools refer ninety percent of the children. We have grown to such an extent that the Institute has an Executive Director, three paid experienced teachers who diagnose the children's learning problems as well as train and assist the approximately one hundred fifteen volunteer reading and writing coaches. The children are tested every six months to monitor their progress and the results have been promising. It has been wonderful to see children begin to believe they can learn and to see the joy the coaches experience when they see significant growth. The coaches, who are all volunteers, build rapport with the children and some stay on two or three years with the same child.

In the first two years as Director, I was devoting sixty-five hours a week to the Institute and did almost everything. I tested the children, trained the volunteer coaches, led the groups and tutored. I cut back to approximately twenty hours a week after I retired from serving as Executive Director. I then served on the Board of Directors, tutored two students, and wrote grant proposals for funding. The Executive Director of the Institute recently resigned and I was asked to take over the role on an interim basis. I have presently committed to serving as a volunteer Director for six months.

Founders need to know when to start letting go and allow others to take over. That was also the case with another organization, Young Peoples Theatre (YPT), which I founded in 1977. YPT sponsors acting classes and theatre productions for school age children. It is still going strong and over time others have taken on the responsibilities for running it. My youngest son, Rick, whose interest in theatre motivated me to start YPT, is now a professional actor as well as the founder and director of the Mosaic Youth Theatre of Detroit. He says watching me found YPT made him believe that he could start Mosaic Youth Theatre, that I was a role model for him.

My husband, Larry, and I have three other children: Mike is an attorney and has his own law firm in Milwaukee; Anne is a scientist and an associate professor on the University of Chicago faculty; and Gene is an economist. Gene was President Clinton's National Economic Advisor and was head of the National Economic Council from 1996-2000. He was with Clinton for eight years.

We have nine grandchildren and every summer we run "Sperling Summer Camp" for them. They come to stay with us for one to two weeks and every day we do activities that the children plan. Initially, I started it as a gift to my children to give them vacation time but it has become a gift to us as we have bonded with our grandchildren and they have bonded with one another.

I've always been a high-energy person. I still get a lot done in a day and can go, go, go, on a project, although I now can feel fatigue at the end of the day. That's new for me. There is a joke going around that I asked my husband, "Is this how normal people feel?" I'm in good health but I do have osteoporosis. I play tennis throughout the year, belong to a book club and I've taken up playing bridge again. I'm also taking a Spanish class since my new daughter-in-law comes from Mexico. When I "really retire," I'd like to play the piano, paint, do photography, read more and become more computer literate.

Once a replacement for the Executive Director position is found, I again need to put lots of time into fundraising for the Institute. I want to be sure it is on more solid ground. I also have some challenges I want to pursue, advocating with the schools for some classes and programs needed by the children we have tutored. It doesn't end when the children leave us. There will always be something to fight for. You are never done, just the way it is with your own children.

Ann Arbor, Michigan

Doris Sperling was born in 1931 in Mount Vernon, New York, and raised in Miami Beach, Florida. She is a graduate of the University of Michigan's School of Art and has a Masters Degree in Education. She met her husband at the beginning of her freshman year of college and they were married on graduation day. Larry, a lawyer, is still in practice. Doris has received numerous awards in recognition of her community service.

Kenneth Lajoie
Age 66
Geologist and Amateur Archeologist for
Egyptian Archeological Excavations

Retirement enabled me to do something I had put off and dreamed about—participating in archeological excavations. I am fortunate that my expertise in geology opened the door for me to ancient Egyptian archeology. I have to pinch myself when I sit on the Wall of the Crow overlooking the Giza Pyramids. It is so exciting to be on a site of such magnitude and magnetism.

When I was an undergraduate at Berkeley I actually took more courses in archeology and anthropology than in geology. It was a toss-up which direction I would go when I graduated. The job market was better in geology so I decided to go that route and I got a Ph.D. at Berkeley and then went on to post-graduate training at Columbia. I started working for the United States Geological Survey in 1970 and worked for the U.S.G.S. for thirty years. I retired at the age of sixty in 2000. Throughout my professional career I sought out and collaborated with archeologists.

I started working at the U.S.G.S. at the beginning of the growth expansion in California. There were many real estate developments taking place on active fault lines and on unsafe and unstable marine coastlines and flood plains. The U.S.G.S. received funding from HUD (the Department of Housing and Urban Development) to look into these problems and advise them, as they were backing a lot of home loans. This project became the focus of my work. I concentrated on the flatlands of the San Francisco Bay Area and issues of seismic safety. We generated a series of maps of hazards

41

to be used in developmental planning. I also worked closely with various public agencies at all levels—city, county, state and national—trying to incorporate scientific information into the planning process. I was committed to the use of scientific information for societal needs. We had some impact when providing information about hazards for critical structures such as nuclear reactors or natural gas facilities. But in many situations, when economics came into the picture, economics won over science. So my personal take is that though the work had some impact, a lot of the information was ignored or not adequately used.

At one point in my career I thought I would never retire, that I would die at my desk. A "perfect storm" of federal agency collapse due primarily to politics and cuts in funding, in addition to a lack of clarity of agency mission, led me to shift my thinking about retirement. I started thinking and dreaming about archeology.

A number of years before retiring, I began giving slide lectures on the geology of the San Francisco Bay Area. I initially started these lectures as a way to combat some bad science that was being done. I then expanded the presentations to address many different audiences, from scientists to schoolchildren. I incorporated a good deal of archeology in the lectures, as audiences were interested in the remains of early human habitation and the large extinct animals that had been in the area. I continued the talks after I retired. They have generated a good deal of interest and I've given between two hundred and three hundred presentations thus far. It has become part of my persona.

I actively sought out archeological groups and one of my presentations was to a small archeological consulting firm, Tremaine and Associates. This led to the firm asking me to do some geological work for them. In 2003, Mark Lehner, a prominent Egyptologist, and Zahee Hawass, chief of Egypt's Supreme Council of Antiquities, hired Tremaine to use a geophysical exploration tool they had developed to locate buried structures beneath the ground. Hawass and Lehner were working on Giza Plateau excavations near the pyramids. Hawass was excavating a village inhabited by the laborers who built the pyramids. Mark Lehner had expanded the research

to a site that they thought was inhabited by the people who directed the construction. Tremaine and Associates needed someone with geological expertise and hired me. They didn't know at the time that I had been doing some research on my own on ancient Egypt. I got to work with Mark Lehner and I let him know that I would be happy to volunteer as an amateur archeologist, as well as a geologist. He took me up on my offer.

Just recently, a geological problem came up and he asked me to work on it as soon as possible. A trench that encroaches on an archeological site was bulldozed by mistake. The trench exposed geological strata with flood and archeological deposits he would like studied. It needs to be done immediately as the trench must be refilled. So I'm in the process of getting ready to leave for Egypt in a few days. I plan to write an article about the geology of the trench after I have finished the work. I'd also like to publish a reevaluation of radiocarbon dates from samples that were taken from first to twelfth dynasty monuments. The dating needs to be reworked and the samples have been made available to me. I hope I can go back to "playing" archeologist in the future and do so for many years. But even doing geology there is exciting.

There are other sites in the world I would love to work on as well, particularly Catal Huyak in Turkey. I hoped something like this would happen when I contacted and started making presentations to archeological groups. It worked out better than I ever thought it would and I'm very fortunate that this dream has come true.

My wife, Andrea, and I have traveled extensively and love prehistory. There are sites around the world that excite us and give us chills; places such as Petra and Mycenae. Andrea is a good researcher, we are a good team, and we do the research on Egypt together. It is a shared interest and her contributions help me a lot. When I'm in Egypt, I communicate with Andrea by e-mail and keep her updated on my work. She then sends those communications on to friends and family who are interested in what I'm doing. So many people are fascinated by my work in Egypt.

We are both in good health. We exercise and pay attention to what we eat. I still backpack, cycle and go kayaking although I have slowed down and don't have the same stamina I used to have. Neither of us sits around and laments the fact that we are slowing down. We just know that the older we get the more we have to work hard on staying fit and healthy. We realize how fortunate we are as we have friends with serious medical problems. Our parents were no longer healthy at our age.

We have two sons, one daughter-in-law and two granddaughters. We look upon our granddaughters, who are now sixteen and seventeen years old, as our second family. We see them often and take them on trips with us to Europe as well as on trips in the States. We used to backpack and hike with our sons when they were young. Now we do that with our granddaughters. Once they got old enough we started taking them along with us on our fishing and camping trips. It has been a pleasure to have them as part of our lives and to introduce them to new experiences and teach them new skills.

Menlo Park, California

Kenneth Lajoie was born in Maine in 1939 and moved to California with his family when he was eleven years old. He spent his senior year of high school in Bangladesh (then East Pakistan), where his father was an engineer on a hydroelectric project. His wife, Andrea, is a former schoolteacher. They met in high school and were high school sweethearts.

Marilynn Rosenthal
Age 75
Author of *9/11: Searching for My Son and His Killers*
Professor Emerita of Sociology
Adjunct Professor of Internal Medicine
University of Michigan

My son, Joshua, age forty-four, a senior vice president and investment portfolio manager for Fiduciary Trust Company International, was on the 94th floor of the south tower of the World Trade Center when the second hijacked plane slammed into it on September 11th. After Josh's death, I became obsessed with the need to find out and understand what happened. Initially, the attack seemed to have come out of the blue, but of course once you looked at it, it wasn't like that at all. There was a larger context and I wanted to comprehend it.

There was so much I needed to find out and understand and I saw the process of researching and writing a book as a way to do that. A few days after we knew Josh had died, a cousin of mine, who is an excellent journalist, called to talk. In the course of the conversation, he asked how I felt about the fact that what was happening to me was also happening to the country and had national significance. I think that clicked in my mind as it went along with what I was already thinking. I think my obsession with understanding is also a reflection of my profession. I'm a trained sociologist and sociologists always want to look beneath the surface. I had done extensive research and written or edited eight books during my academic career so that researching and writing a book on 9/11 was, in a way, a continuation of that career. I also realized I had the skills to do this and most 9/11 families don't have these skills.

All the 9/11 family members I've met wanted to know where their loved ones were at the time of the attack. Although I wanted to know a lot more, I certainly wanted to know where Josh was that morning. Fortunately, I was able to find that out right away. Josh's company had a memorial service for its eighty-six members who died and at the service I met the last person to see Josh. He was a Japanese businessman, a client, and Josh had put him on the elevator when the first tower was hit. The man made himself available to me and I spoke with him at length, two or three times, as I couldn't take it all in at one time.

Very early on, I had a sense that the pilot, Marwan al-Shehhi, who crashed the plane into Josh's tower, was another mother's son. He was twenty-three years old at the time and from the United Arab Emirates. I recall hearing Theodore Olson, then the U.S. Solicitor General, whose wife died in the Pentagon crash, talking on the radio and referring to the hijackers as savages and animals who hated our democracy. I thought that was an unfortunate way to think of them; they were human beings and other mothers' sons. Why did I think that? I really don't know but it was a strong feeling from the beginning. It made it possible for me to look at this young man's life in a relatively open way. Marwan al-Shehhi has become a big part of my life. I probably know this boy better in some ways than his own mother.

As I started doing research, I began to think about the two men, my son and Marwan, who died together and what brought them to the 94th floor of the south tower of the World Trade Center on 9/11? In the course of my investigation, I realized that I was dealing with two different worlds that were related to one another and, of course, clashed. I organized the book around the two biographies, which are meant to be emblematic, not only of the lives of the individuals but of two global movements. Josh was part of the American world of finance that has been globalized and Marwan was part of the global Islamist, jihadist movement. Marwan was a *true believer* and died for what he considered to be a good cause. In the process he was, of course, a murderer. I use the stories of the men to tell about the movements and the variety of ways the two worlds have touched one another, not just on 9/11.

I got information for the book from a variety of sources. B.K.A., the German equivalent of our F.B.I., had extensive interrogation files on the Hamburg cell, which included considerable information on Marwan. I obtained access to the translated B.K.A. files at the law firm representing the 9/11 families who are suing the Saudi charities for financing Al Qaeda. There were all sorts of other media sources. I thought of visiting Marwan's family in the United Arab Emirates from the very beginning and finally was able to make an eight-day visit in August 2005. The American Ambassador and UAE officials were very helpful in facilitating the visit. I was able to meet with members of the family, although Marwan's mother and half-brother, who is head of the family, wouldn't meet with me. They've never talked to anyone. It was a good experience to meet with people who have human feelings beyond the pronouncements of government. We treated each other as individuals and I was an honored guest in their homes. They knew I was Jewish. The family members officially don't believe that Marwan did this. But deep down they know he did and they struggle to understand why. Just as I do.

I've recently finished writing the book and feel that I've accomplished my goal. I know a lot more and I understand the context in which Josh died. My research has also made me angry, as I don't think my son had to die or that 9/11 had to happen. There was so much governmental incompetence, so many threat warnings and other information that was ignored or set aside. The book's title is *9/11: Searching for My Son and His Killers.* In researching the book, I was not only searching to learn about Marwan but also searching for my son on a number of different levels, including finding out about him as an adult making his way in his world.

I'm working with an agent now and I'm discovering that the world of commercial publishing is very different from scholarly publishing. The royalties, when the book is published, will go to the Joshua Rosenthal Memorial Fund, which I helped establish at the Gerald R. Ford School of Public Policy at the University of Michigan. I felt it appropriate that the university Josh attended have a memorial lecture series that brings in experts to lecture on issues related to 9/11. Josh's remains were never found, there is no gravestone—so this is a concrete, living memorial to him.

The second thing I strongly felt, in addition to needing to understand why 9/11 happened, was that it was important for me and for my family to get our lives back. We were all devastated, particularly my daughter, Helen; but I thought it important that this not dominate the rest of our lives, that we not become a professional 9/11 family.

Beyond writing the book, which of course had not been part of my plan for this time in my life, I wanted to be able to go back to teaching and scholarly work. My career started late and I didn't get my Ph.D. until age forty-five. I've enjoyed my work immensely, found it interesting and challenging, and wanted to get back to it. My health is reasonably good and my mind is functioning. I retired from the University of Michigan at Dearborn two years ago at age seventy-three. I was a professor, a medical sociologist and director of the Program in Health Policy Studies. I no longer teach full-time and I now have an adjunct appointment in the Department of Internal Medicine in the Medical School in Ann Arbor. My research in patient safety and medical mistakes led to the appointment. I teach short seminars in the Medical School as well as a class for premedical students in the Liberal Arts College entitled *Becoming a Doctor: More than a Science.*

I think another reason why I felt so strongly about the need for us to get back to our lives has to do with my family background and the losses I've experienced. I was the youngest of four sisters and one of my sisters died when I was eight years old. My parents never recovered from her death and it marked the rest of their lives as well as our family life. In addition to Josh, I lost another son, Daniel, whose death in 1977 at the age of twenty, was due to a defective heart valve. I was determined to not handle their deaths the way my parents had handled my sister's death.

Ann Arbor, Michigan

Marilynn Rosenthal (b. 1930) is a native of Detroit. She received a B.A. degree from Wayne State University and a Ph.D. from the University of Michigan. She is divorced and her daughter, son-in-law and two granddaughters live in New York City. Marilynn has a large extended family as well as a large circle of friends.

Jai-Zhen Song
Age 71
Composer and Conductor

In 1982, at the age of forty-seven, I left a successful music career in China and immigrated to the United States with my wife and two daughters. My wife's entire family, grandparents, parents and siblings, had gradually, one by one, immigrated to the United States and settled in New York City. She was the only one in her family left in China; she missed them and was unhappy. I wanted her to be happy so we gave up our life in China so she could be reunited with her family. We also thought coming to this country would enable our daughters to get a good education.

It was a very hard time for me. Music had been my career in China and for seven years (1982-1989) I worked at ten different non-music jobs so we could survive. These included employment as a cafeteria worker, janitor, house and office cleaner, home attendant, garment worker, phone receptionist for Chinese organizations and editor for a Chinese language newspaper. I didn't give up music entirely however, as I conducted the Chinese National Orchestra and a choir on a part-time basis on weekends. My wife had been a physician in China, but she never practiced medicine in the States because she wasn't able to pass the exams, due to the language barrier. She ended up working in the garment industry.

In 1989, I was diagnosed with chronic myelocytic leukemia. In a ten-year period I had twelve hospital stays and seven surgeries. During my hospitalizations I returned to composing and I think music saved my life. I poured out all my feelings of pain, fear, homesickness and loneliness into the music. I finished two compositions while lying in a hospital bed in

Sloan-Kettering Cancer Center. The Chinese National Orchestra performed them for the first time in 1992 at Merkin Concert Hall in New York City. I was in the hospital undergoing a bone marrow transplant operation at the time. In 1995, I compiled a songbook entitled *Songs for a Man Away From Home*. All the pieces were composed while I was in the hospital.

I was born in the Guongxi Autonomous Region of China, an area renowned for its folk songs. My family lived in the countryside. They were educated people but no one in the family had an interest in the arts—music, dancing or painting. When I was fourteen years old, I was chosen by the local arts association to study music. I learned how to play the trumpet, French horn and accordion and studied music theory. The emphasis was on Western instruments and Western music. At the age of seventeen, I became interested in composing and both taught myself and received tutoring from my music director. I was selected to go to Beijing for two years (1955-1957) and to Shanghai for another two years (1961-1963) to receive professional training. The best students from around the country trained in these programs. I learned a great deal in those four years.

After the training, the students were all sent back to their provinces to work. I was inducted into the Chinese Musical Association at that time. The years of the Cultural Revolution, which followed, were not too hard on me. It took a toll on people who were prominent and older. I was a young man in my thirties and I wasn't given any hard physical labor. I did have to stop composing for a number of years and I had no choice but to do the jobs assigned to me.

At a later time, I was assigned to art organizations in different provinces and was able to work professionally as a composer and conductor. While touring in the provinces as a conductor, I started collecting folksongs. Folk music became a source of musical inspiration for me. I proceeded to study Chinese music and began to integrate traditional Chinese music with Western music, which I continue to do to this day.

In 2000, the Chinese Musical Society, sponsored by the New York Chapter of Chinese Americans, featured my music in a concert in honor of my fifty years of dedication to music. The concert was entitled *Nostalgic*

Songs of China. The songs are an expression of longing for my parents, for China and for the past.

I presently compose, arrange, and conduct music. I leave pencils and papers all around my house, including the bathroom, so when I have an inspiration I can write it down right away and not lose it. My compositions are for both choral and instrumental music. Most of my composing is done in my head although I use an electric keyboard when I transcribe. I write the lyrics for my choral music; I've also rewritten lyrics for Chinese popular songs. The lyrics are in Mandarin. I can speak Cantonese, as my wife is Cantonese, but I write in Mandarin. I think my music is easy to recognize; when you hear it you know it is mine. In addition to composing, I presently conduct two choirs. Right now, I'm arranging the music for one of them. Due to its popularity, the Senior Chorus of the City Hall Senior Center of Hamilton-Madison House, which I conduct, performs an increasing number of concerts for the community each year.

In addition to music, I write poetry and do calligraphy. My father taught me calligraphy and I've been doing it for a long time. I used to enjoy participating in sports when I was young; now I swim three or four times a week to stay fit. I go for regular medical checkups and take ten pills a day to keep me healthy.

My wife and I have now been married for forty-five years. Our two daughters are college graduates; the older daughter is a New York City middle school teacher and our younger daughter is an economist employed by a bank. Our daughters are married, we have four grandchildren, and they all live in New York. My family has been a great source of support to me.

I would love to be able to go back to China one day and have the total body of my work performed there. That is my dream.

New York City

(My special thanks to Chao-hong Feng for her assistance as interpreter.)

Author's Note: I located Mr. Song via a chain of referrals. I requested the assistance of a well-connected friend in New York City who is a professor of Social Work. I told her about my project and my interest in locating people of diverse racial and ethnic backgrounds. She referred me to a colleague, who suggested I talk to the director of the City Hall Senior Center of Hamilton-Madison House. She, in turn, referred me to one of her staff members. That staff member then arranged for me to meet Mr. Song, the Center's choir director.

The Center is located in Manhattan's Lower East Side near Chinatown, and serves a large Chinese clientele. I ended up spending two days at the Center and it was a fascinating experience. It is a vibrant and busy place with numerous activities going on at the same time. While I was there I was aware of dancing, exercise and Tai Chi classes. I could hear the clinking of tiles in the busy mahjong room, saw ping pong and chess games in progress, observed a much used library with Chinese language books and newspapers, and watched a class in traditional Chinese painting being taught by a prominent painter, Wenyu Li. A full lunch, with many Chinese dishes, was served at noon and the dining room was packed.

Jai-Zhen Song doesn't speak English, or perhaps he didn't feel his English was adequate, and the Center arranged for a Mandarin/English interpreter, Chao-hong Feng, to join us. This was a new experience for me, as I don't recall ever conducting an interview with an interpreter. Chao-hong Feng is a member of one of Mr. Song's choirs, and she commented to me that she thought he was a talented, generous and courageous man. There was a very good natured feeling among the three of us as we searched for the right words to convey intent and meaning. Although I am sure some things were lost in translation, I think for the most part we were able to understand one another. After the interview, both Jai-Zhen Song and Chao-hong Feng insisted that I join them for lunch at the Center. After the meal, they asked a passerby to take snapshots of the three of us together, as they both wanted a memento of the meeting.

A few months after our interview, I heard from Chao-hong Feng that Mr. Song was leaving for a trip to China. I think it may have been his first trip back since he emigrated. I hope his dream to have his work performed in China will become a reality.

Carleen McGinn
Age 81
Stephen Minister

I tell the church groups that I talk to that I think there are two kinds of healers, the wounded healers and the blessed healers. The wounded healers are persons who come from turbulent family backgrounds and/or have experienced significant losses in their lives. By going into the healing professions, they not only help others but they seek to heal and to understand themselves. I believe I'm one of the blessed healers because of my family background. My parents, and particularly my father, who was a theologian and Methodist minister, always sent a clear message to me as well as to my younger sister. The message was that you couldn't have a relationship with God, this wonderful being, larger than anybody could imagine, without relationships with people. And that meant that you were to serve. My parents demonstrated that message in the way they lived their lives.

As a result, it was natural that I wanted to do something that helped others. Initially, I couldn't decide between a career in music therapy or social work but after teaching in an elementary school in a cotton mill town in South Carolina, I decided on social work. I received my social work training at Tulane University and worked as a clinical social worker at the Family and Children's Service in Nashville, Tennessee, a United Way Agency, for thirty-seven years. I was Director of Professional Services for seventeen years and was in that position in 1989 when I reached the retirement age of sixty-five.

I was aware that I was going to have all this time in retirement, I still had enthusiasm for clinical work and helping people and I started thinking about private practice. A social work friend, in fact, someone I had once supervised, who had a private office, said, "You come on and use the office here and you can teach us more about family therapy." I started working one day a week but soon found I had so many clients that I increased my work time to two days a week, scheduling six to eight sessions a day. My clientele included people who might not have gone to Family and Children's Services for help—professionals in the music industry and gay and lesbian clients. I worked with some gay and lesbian clients when I first started private practice and they got the word out about me. I think the fact that I was a straight older woman, church affiliated, with strong southern roots, yet accepting of their sexual orientation, was important.

I retired a second time in 2002, not because of lack of enthusiasm for the work, but because I was seventy-eight and my husband, Bruce, was eighty-three years old. I worried that I would suddenly have to leave my clients if something happened to one of us. As a result, I gradually started "graduating" and transferring my clientele.

During that transitional time, I was asked if I was interested in becoming a Stephen Minister in our church, the West End United Methodist Church in Nashville. I thought this was a way in which I could still use my skills and have back-up if anything happened to Bruce or me. That, and my commitment to the church, made for a good fit.

A Lutheran Minister, who was also a clinical psychologist, developed Stephen Ministry, now a movement in mainstream Protestant Churches. A Stephen Minister is a congregation member who listens in a compassionate, non-judgmental way, and is committed to providing confidential one-on-one Christian care to individuals facing difficulties in their lives. They can discuss religious concerns and pray with the care receivers but they are not therapists, advice givers or problem solvers. We have fourteen Stephen Ministers in our church, serving a congregation of two thousand. Referrals come from our minister as well as former care receivers.

Despite my clinical experience, I still needed to complete over fifty hours of training in Christian caregiving as well as additional leadership training. It was a pretty easy transfer because of my religious background. I can now talk about spiritual and religious issues and pray with people, things I couldn't do in my clinical practice. I might have prayed by myself before going into a therapeutic interview but I never would have prayed with a client. So it has been freeing for me.

Both of my initial trainers at the church were former clients of mine and they were very appreciative of the skills I could bring to the program. As a result, I've played a special, and much needed, role in helping with the selection of new Stephen Ministers as well as monitoring those new to the program. Screening for the right people is so important as not everyone is a good listener or can put themselves in another person's shoes. I am now a leader and facilitator of one of the two peer supervision groups, which inevitably involves providing additional consultation and support outside of the group meetings. Another special role I play is assisting in making referrals when care receivers need professional help. In addition to those responsibilities, I am presently working with two care receivers.

It is gratifying to me when I help others muster their strengths and abilities and I can assist them in finding hope. It is also satisfying when I teach new skills to Stephen Ministry volunteers, which they can use in the helping process. Being a Stephen Minister has enabled me to merge together my professional clinical skills and my religious beliefs and background.

There were many years in my adult life when I was not active in the church. This was not because of a lack of faith but rather because I questioned the church as an institution and some of its policies. Eight years ago, I became so angry at the policy of the National General Conference of the Methodist Church towards homosexuals that I decided to again become involved and work for change. I've been a member of a church group working for openness and inclusion and we have made considerable progress.

My father, as a minister in small South Carolina communities, set a model for me in the way he fought for civil rights and inclusion of African-Americans in the church. My father was a Turberville, from the town by the same name, and I've always been proud of being a Turberville. In retrospect, I wish I had kept the name when I married and kept the line going. I knew I wanted to marry a good man like my father and my uncle Archie, who was also a minister. But I didn't want to marry a minister, because as a minister's daughter I felt I lived in a fishbowl. I did achieve what I wanted when I married Bruce and we have now been married for fifty-five years.

I try to stay fit by doing strength training and working with a nutritionist. I used to walk a lot but have had to stop because of repetitive fractures in one foot and arthritis in my knee. I'm scheduled for knee replacement surgery and hope I can resume walking once I recover.

I enjoy reading, music, good movies and travel. Most of all I treasure friends and family.

Nashville, Tennessee

Carleen McGinn was born (1924) and raised in South Carolina. She and her husband, Bruce, a retired banker, have been long-time residents of Nashville. Their immediate family includes their two sons, Wilson and David, their sons' wives, Denise and Elaine, and their grandson, Philip.

Fay Kleinman
Age 94
Artist

Why am I getting more and more ideas now for paintings (and writing) than I've ever had before? I'd like to know the answer to that. Is it because time is short and I instinctively know that, so something is moving faster in me? I was never robust and I'm surprised I'm still here. I think it is willpower. I still have so many ideas I have to stick around to do them.

I was born in 1912 and was drawing all the time as a child. The most important fact in my life was the encouragement my mother and father gave me. The amount of praise was tremendous. I wanted to do more each time and get more praise. Both of my parents were dressmakers and they did beautiful, artistic work. My parents allowed me to take materials and drape them over dressmaker dummies so my feeling for design started early.

I wanted to be a nurse when I graduated from high school and I applied to Bellevue Hospital but was told there was a wait of three years. I guess fate was at work. A good friend, who is still with us, said, "You are always talking about painting, so do it." She gave me my first paint set and told me about the free art classes sponsored by the W.P.A. (Works Progress Administration). And that's how I got started.

I later won a scholarship to the American Artists School. I didn't realize then how many well-known artists were teaching there and I was allowed to take classes with any teacher I wanted. I also took courses at the National Academy of Design and studied sculpture at City College. I had my first exhibit when I was still an art student. I later exhibited at a number of well-known art galleries in New York City. There were so many things I wanted to do; writing was one of them and I took courses in short story writing. To this day, I inundate the world with hundreds of poems and stories. I have lots of writing projects going on right now.

I was lucky to have been married to two extraordinary men. My first husband, Jack Skurnick, was a record producer; he founded EMS Recording. He was also a music critic. He died of a heart attack at the age of forty-one in 1952. I was only thirty-nine years old at the time and had a young daughter, Davi, to raise. I married my second husband, Emanuel Levenson, seven years later. Jack, Emanuel and I had all been good friends. Emanuel was a concert pianist and opera director. He died in 1998.

Emanuel and I decided to move to the Berkshires. I had lived in New York for fifty years and we ended up living in Massachusetts for the next twenty-five years. We started the Becket Art Center there and it is still going strong. By now they have forgotten me and don't even know who started it. My first exhibit in Massachusetts was in Becket in 1969. After that I exhibited my work in many museums and galleries in the state.

We moved to Michigan in 1986 at the urging of my daughter and her family who were living here. I've continued to paint and I'm still changing and experimenting and doing different work. Over the years I've been inspired and influenced by different artists and styles but I think my own style comes from what I feel, which gets expressed in my painting. My subject matter varies and influences my style as well. In both my painting and writing, I'm serious some of the time, whimsical at other times, as if I can't make up my mind. But in the end it is pretty much all *me*.

I love painting from life better than anything although I also like painting from my imagination. Right now, I'm doing more abstract, non-objective painting, working with color. I'm presently preparing for an exhibit entitled *Ordinary People* that will soon open at the Ann Arbor Public Library.

I hadn't planned to continue exhibiting when we moved to Michigan but due to the encouragement and support of others, I've had a number of shows here. The Ypsilanti Library recently bought one of my pieces for their permanent collection after my exhibit there.

A number of years ago, I illustrated a book of haiku, *Three Line Words* by David Latner, published in 2001. I'm now working on illustrating a book of my own haiku poems entitled *Mrrow*. I wrote and collected the poems ten years ago, and due to the urging of a friend, I've been adding illustrations to it this past year. I would love to get the book published. I'm also working on a number of children's stories (which are not yet finished) and on a children's book about color. I am often asked, "How do you get your color?" I was first asked that by a teacher watching me paint. I did not quite understand his question at the time but I answered, "Well, I see it." And that's still the answer. The idea for the book about color came to me after I was asked that question at an exhibit reception.

My mind is going all the time, even when I sleep. When I'm not having nightmares, I dream about pictures in color as well as stories. When I can't sleep, I write, although painting is my most steady activity. I have no work schedule; I work for different periods at different times—less now, depending on how I feel. At no time did I ever paint for a lot of hours. The most I've done is three hours at a time. Painting is such an intense experience; I'm in another world, it is a magical experience and I can't sustain it for very long. I'm not good at talking about my paintings and I'm not comfortable talking about myself. I depend on my paintings to talk for me. Exhibiting is a mixed experience for me as I'm shy to begin with and exhibiting is showing myself. To know me is to see me through my paintings.

Ypsilanti, Michigan

Fay Kleinman was born and raised in New York City, the younger of two children of Russian immigrants. Her older brother was an architect. She is the mother of Davi Napolean and grandmother of Brian and Randy (a well-known jazz guitarist). Both her daughter and son-in-law, Greg Napolean, are very supportive of her work and Greg frames her paintings. Her work is represented in many collections, here and abroad. Fay has written her memoirs and addressed them to her daughter, Davi.

Robert L. Kahn
Age 87
Co-Author of *Successful Aging*
Professor Emeritus of Psychology and Public Health
Research Scientist Emeritus,
Institute for Social Research
University of Michigan

I retired in 1988 at the age of seventy, as that was the legal requirement at the time. I think that even if it hadn't been a requirement, I would have made some changes in what I was doing. First of all, the University's Institute of Social Research (ISR), which has been my main home for half a century or more, is essentially a soft-money operation. For decades, I felt responsible for supporting a staff, and for helping to maintain the Survey Research Center, a unit within ISR. Academic money raising takes a great deal of time and energy and I no longer wanted to make that kind of energy investment, at least in raising money. I would have done something different, exactly what I don't know.

I had some hobby-related ideas. I thought I might improve my carpentry to the level of cabinet-making or perhaps restore an old car (a dream of many a Detroit boy). I used to play the piano and I thought of taking piano lessons and becoming reasonably proficient.

None of these things happened. About the time of my retirement, the John D. and Catherine T. MacArthur Foundation was putting together a multi-disciplinary effort to examine aging. My research on stress in organizational life, which had led to studies of stress in general and its physical and medical consequences, as well as the factors that mitigated or buffered the effects of stress, interested the MacArthur people. I was invited to join the multi-disciplinary group of scholars they were assembling and whose research they planned to finance for ten years. I accepted the invitation and this changed the direction of my research life. The group was made up of sixteen scholars representing the disciplines relevant to aging. Like most of the group, I was not a gerontologist, but it was not too much of a strain to become one. I was already developing an old man's interest in gerontology.

I began a whole new life. Not only was the research new for me, the collaboration with physicians and geneticists was new for me as well. It was intellectually exciting and it also got me in touch with a group of relatively young people. It is marvelous in your old age to acquire a bunch of young exciting colleagues and to be interacting with them.

The MacArthur Foundation officers wanted us to be innovative. After some investigation, we decided not to concentrate on what people lose, decade by decade, as they age. That has been well documented. We decided instead to look at the differences between people in old age and determine the factors that enabled individuals who function effectively, both physically and mentally, to do so. Our research projects looked at these factors, leading to a departure from a disease framework of aging toward a positive model that we called "successful aging." Roget's *Thesaurus* defines "success" as flourishing or doing well, which is why we used the term. By successful aging, we meant the ability to maintain three main characteristics: low risk of disease or disease-related disability, high mental and physical functioning, and active engagement in life.

The findings of our various research projects were published in a variety of scientific journals but little effort had been made to make them accessible to a wider audience. We thought, as the ten-year period of MacArthur support was ending, that the findings should be brought together and made available to the public. John Rowe and I decided that we would take a shot at it and that led to the book *Successful Aging*, which was published in 1998, with a paperback edition in 1999. The book has done quite well and we have the second edition ready to go. It brings the research up to date and includes some new topics. For example, the first

edition did not deal with issues of religion and spirituality. We had been criticized for that omission, and we have added new chapters on the topic based on data we now have.

I've also had the opportunity to study the application of some of the strategies for successful aging that came out of the research. A former financial officer of the MacArthur Foundation, who now heads a corporation that owns and operates retirement communities in Florida, wanted to introduce a program to increase successful aging in those communities. A program was set up on an experimental basis in two communities, with research to assess its effects. Increased exercise facilities, information about diet, and assistance from a trained lifestyle coordinator were some of the services provided. We developed measures of health, physical and mental functioning, life satisfaction and mobility. Mayo Clinic provided online measures of medical and behavioral risk factors. Measurements were taken at the beginning of the program and then at six months, twelve months and now annually.

The findings have been interesting, although not exactly what we expected. The functional level of residents in our experimental group, who are in their eighties, remained stable or showed modest improvement. I became more excited about these results when I looked at the national data, which showed that octogenarians' functional level plunged, even for those in the highest educational and socio-economic group. So the fact that octogenarians in our group remained stable or improved slightly is cause for celebration. Colleagues in this program have now set up a non-profit company, making the material we have developed available to other retirement communities.

I continue to be involved in that work and I enjoy it. But I'm not working as hard as I used to. ISR provides me with an office and occasional secretarial help, for which I am grateful. I usually get to the office at 9:30 a.m.—a civilized hour. Three days a week, I leave the office at 1:30 p.m. and go to the recreation center to work out. I used to run and bench press my weight, now I walk the track and lift less ambitious weights. I'm committed to staying fit and have been since I began to show symptoms of hypertension and cardiac problems at an early age. My parents died young from these problems. Diet, medication and exercise have enabled me to control them. During the summer, I continue the aerobics and weight-lifting, and I also swim and sail. I have an old sloop and a few years ago I purchased a Sunfish, a little sailboat that I can easily handle by myself.

I'd say that the most important relationships in my life now are my family, but that has always been true. My wife, Bea, and I have been married for sixty-five years and we know we are fortunate to be together. We are very close to our three daughters, our four grandchildren and our son-in-law, Erik Wright. But I've also had some beautiful, almost lifelong, friendships. The sad thing, if you live long enough, is that you lose your oldest friends. That is an unavoidable pain of old age. Such friends are irreplaceable, although I enjoy and am deeply grateful for the friendship of younger people.

I have also become a letter writer in my old age. I have a lovely correspondence with my granddaughter, Becky, which has almost become a hobby. Eight years ago, she decided that instead of giving Bea and me a Christmas gift, she would write to us once a month. She was a senior in high school then and she's now doing graduate work at the University of London. She's written every month and her letters are both personal and very literary, reflecting her reading and thinking. Her letters have revived my old literary interests. I answer them and we now have a great collection of these paired letters, almost two hundred of them. The correspondence has become a lovely part of my life; it has stimulated my reading and also led me to write to other people. Letter writing may be an 18th-century habit, but the 18th century wasn't called the "Enlightenment" by mistake.

Ann Arbor, Michigan

Robert Kahn (b. 1918) grew up in Detroit, Michigan. He received a B.A. degree in English in 1939 and a Ph.D. in Social Psychology in 1952, both from the University of Michigan. He is recognized as a leading scholar in survey research and organizational behavior and is the author or co-author of four books in those fields, in addition to the book on successful aging.

3

Fine Arts, Crafts, Performing Arts
and Physical Accomplishments

This chapter contains the stories of those taking the third and fourth paths. These paths involve the further development or flourishing of avocations, and the start of brand new endeavors. The primary activities presented in this chapter are in the arts, although athletic accomplishments are also included. Community service was an important secondary activity for some of the artists. Community service as a primary activity is presented in chapter four.

Several avocations were long-standing, going back to childhood or teenage years. Other avocations started when individuals were in their fifties, the decade prior to traditional retirement, and sometimes there was not a clear demarcation between the late developing avocations and new beginnings. As we look at these later developing avocations and new endeavors, we often see the fulfillment of long-held dreams, the blossoming of latent talents, as well as the use of creative expression to cope with adversity and loss.

1. Miriam Brysk
   Multi-Media Artist
   Author of *Shattered Childhood*

2. John Chan
   Photographer

3. Albine Bech
   Tai Chi and Aquatic Exercise Teacher
   Elementary School Tutor

4. Sheldon Markel
   Artist

5. Tyrone Smith
   Leader and Soloist for the Tyrone Smith Revue
   Coach for Middle School Basketball Team

6. Dean Bush
   Maker of Musical Instruments
   Woodworker
   Antique Shop Owner

7. Carrie Lo
   Artist
   Arts and Crafts Teacher

8. David Herzig
   Woodworker
   Pharmaceutical Industry Consultant

9. Laurie Naiman
   Photographer
   Web Site Designer

10. Lois Kivi Nochman
    World Class Master Swimmer

11. Marvin Nochman
    Actor and Director

12. Harry Steinberg
    Sculptor

Miriam Brysk
Age 70
Mixed-Media Artist

Many years have come and gone since then
As I attempt to view my past anew
I try in retrospect to still decipher why
I was spared to live while other children died

From Silent Trees, a poem by Miriam Brysk

I have three obligations as a holocaust survivor: to remember, to teach, and to live the life those killed would have wanted to live.

I was born in Warsaw in 1935 and the war started in 1939. Throughout the war years I was called Mirele (the Yiddish diminutive of Miriam). Then there was a transition into Miriam when we immigrated to the United States. It was a very difficult transition; some aspects of it were even more difficult than the war years. And then I became Dr. Brysk, the scientist and faculty member at the University of Texas Medical Branch, with a CV (professional resume) thirty pages long, totally unlike Mirele or Miriam.

During the war, for a year and a half, my parents and I lived in the Nazi's Jewish ghetto in Lida, in Eastern Poland, now Byelorussia, about two hundred miles from Warsaw. Most of the ghetto's residents were killed in a massive slaughter, similar to the one at Babi Yar. My parents and I were sent to die with the rest of the ghetto population, but because my father was a surgeon, and surgeons were needed, we were spared at the last moment. At first, we thought only my father would survive but my mother and I were also spared. At one point, when there was a rumor that all Jewish children were going to be killed, my parents hid me with a peasant woman outside the town. It was horrible saying goodbye to my parents and not knowing if I would ever see them again. A group of Russian partisans who needed a doctor came and stole us out of the ghetto. My father was the only surgeon at the hospital they set up in a remote part of a forest. We stayed with the partisans for a year and a half and we had some harrowing experiences in the forest as well. To protect me from rape, my head was shaved and I wore boy's clothing. For my eighth birthday, my parents gave me a pistol, which had been taken off a German who had bought it for his girlfriend.

We were liberated by the Russians, but fled them as they wanted to hold on to doctors; and then we made a long trek through Central Europe—through Poland, Czechoslovakia, Hungary, Romania and Austria—until we got to Italy where we remained for two years. My mother had two brothers in Brooklyn who helped us come to the United States and we settled in Brooklyn's Brighton Beach area.

I was twelve when we came to this country and I hated it here. I had no formal schooling, and although I spoke five languages and my parents had taught me to read and write, I spoke no English. I was backwards in many ways and I experienced a lot of cruelty from children who poked fun at me. No one seemed to want to hear about the experiences of holocaust survivors. They seemed to be saying "shut up" in a polite way. This went on for years; no one ever said, "tell me your story." I eventually clammed up.

I progressed rapidly in school and graduated from high school at age seventeen and from New York University at age twenty. I met my husband, Henry, in my sophomore year of college and we got married right before I graduated. He is also a holocaust survivor, from France. He received his Ph.D. in Theoretical Physics when he was twenty-three years old. We moved frequently because of Henry's work, so my graduate studies and post-doctoral fellowships were in many different locations. I received a Master's degree in Bacteriology from the University of Michigan and a Ph.D. in Biological Sciences from Columbia University. My two daughters were born while I was in graduate school. I found it very difficult as a woman to get a tenure track job in a medical school and so I completed three different post-doctoral fellowships. The last one was in dermatology, which became my specialty. I finally got a tenure track position at the University of Texas Medical Branch in Galveston at age forty-four, twelve years after getting my Ph.D. I blossomed professionally, had my own lab, received numerous grants, published frequently, was a full professor in three departments, was on numerous University committees and mentored many female faculty.

Depression haunted me most of my life and it got worse six months after the move to Texas. It felt so unbelievably deep that I couldn't crawl out of it on my own. I went into treatment and stayed in treatment for thirteen years. Therapy enabled me to understand the sources of my depression, to handle things better, to change how I lived and to experience joy. The mother of a friend encouraged me to start painting. I had done some work in photography and always loved art but had no formal art training. I started painting and it helped me let out some of the feelings I wasn't able to express in therapy.

As I neared age sixty-five, I started to contemplate retirement. Henry, who is seven years older than I, had already retired, and was encouraging me to retire as well. We also realized that we wanted to live near our daughters and their families in Michigan. And, frankly, I was getting bored with work; how many times can you keep doing the same thing? Once I retired, I had a glorious sense of freedom. I had never before had that feeling.

Both prior to my retirement and after our move to Michigan, I became enamored with digital art and started learning the techniques, although I wasn't doing anything profound or going in any particular direction with it. I then went on a group trip to visit the former ghettos and concentration camps of Eastern Europe. It was my first trip back and it was unbelievably painful for me to walk into gas chambers. I was overwhelmed by the realization that if not for the partisans, I would have died in one of those chambers. It took a year of incubation after I returned before I started on the artwork I'm now doing. Once I got started, it became an obsession.

My pictures have been described as mixed-media photography collages. The pieces all incorporate photographs of victims of the holocaust taken prior to the war and during the war years. They include photographs of my family; family photographs of other survivors, as well as photographs from books that are in the public domain. The black and white and sepia photographs are all small so I enlarge them using a Xerox machine, transfer the images to watercolor paper, and then scan them into the computer. Thematic material is added, as is color and texture, using different software programs.

For me, the holocaust is a loss of the people. I want to portray them, not as gray shadows walking into gas chambers, but as real people, people with dignity. I want to honor the people who have died and I do it out of a sense of love, not bitterness. Each work concentrates on one individual and his or her plight. All the pictures have an explanatory part to provide context and information about the holocaust. My first exhibit had nineteen pieces, the next one had twenty-seven pieces and my new exhibit has over forty pieces. The body of work is entitled *In a Confined Silence.* I am exhibiting in holocaust museums, as well as other sites around the country and the exhibit is now booked through the next two years. The public response and reviews have been very positive and people report feeling very moved. It has been very fulfilling to me that through my artwork, people are now paying attention to the stories. The next project I'm considering involves transferring holocaust images to fabrics and then adding fringes to create symbolic tallithim (prayer shawls).

Since retirement, in addition to my photography collages, I've completed writing a book. It is an autobiography of the holocaust years and my early years in America. The present title is *Shattered Childhood* and I hope to have it published. I am seventy years old and I don't know how long I will live. I have a sense of urgency to tell the stories of the holocaust, both in my writing and artwork. They need to be recorded before it is too late.

I've been quite healthy, aside from depression, which has been a major problem in my life. I presently go to exercise classes twice a day, morning and evening. I'm a member and on the Board of Directors of a small Jewish congregation—the name translated from Hebrew is Hannah's Orchard. The services are joyful and wonderful and everyone is included. It gives me a sense of meaning. I have never enjoyed my life as much as I do now.

Ann Arbor, Michigan

Miriam Brysk and her husband have been married fifty years. They have two daughters and five grandchildren. Their daughter, Judy, is a gynecologist and their daughter, Havi, is a clinical psychologist.

John Chan
Age 89
Photographer

Retirement was my turning point. I retired in 1980 at the age of sixty-five. I had worked for the California Highway Department, Caltrans, for twenty-nine years as a draftsman and assistant project engineer. Four years before retiring, I started taking art and photography courses at night at both the College of San Mateo and Foothill College. I also attended quite a few photography workshops during those years. I had felt deprived of learning all my life so I tried to catch up.

I was born in Chinatown in San Francisco in 1915, the year of the Pacific Exposition. My mother had emigrated from China and my father was American born. I was the eldest of three children. My mother died when I was seven years old and my father wasn't able to keep the family together. My brother and sister were sent to boarding schools and I went to live with an aunt and uncle and cousins near Chinatown. I saw my siblings often and we remained close. My father lived into his nineties; my sister is living but my brother has passed away.

My interest in art and photography dates back to my early school days when I spent lots of time visiting museums and galleries. I attended the San Francisco Oriental School, a grammar school for Asian students, as we were not allowed to go to school with Caucasians. The policy changed by the time I was in junior high school. I wanted to go to the Polytechnic High School because of the good art program offered there. My junior high school basketball coach was also the coach at Polytechnic and he facilitated my admittance. I took advantage of all the art courses offered in school. I graduated from high school during the Depression and had to work and couldn't go to college. I held a variety of jobs; I sold candy, and did maintenance, restaurant and hotel work. I remained in my aunt and uncle's home until I married my wife, Cecelia, in 1940. We had grown up together and had known one another since grammar school. During World War II, I served in the U.S. Army Signal Corps and later worked for the Navy Department, where I was trained as a draftsman. The training enabled me to get a job at Caltrans.

I received an Associate of Arts Degree in Photography from the College of San Mateo the year I retired. I later entered one of my student photos, a portrait of a young woman, in a contest at the San Mateo County Fair. It won the "Best in the Show" award and that turned my life around. The prize was a one-year tuition scholarship to study photography at the Academy of Art College in San Francisco. When the year ended, the president of the college looked at my portfolio and offered me a full scholarship to get a Bachelor of Fine Arts Degree in Photography. I completed the degree when I was seventy-six years old. I wore the number "76" on the back of my gown when I graduated. Everyone in my family, including my granddaughters, was there.

Since 1980, I've had fifteen solo exhibits and I've participated in a number of group shows. My first solo exhibit was in 1980 at the Canon Gallery in San Francisco. I had gone into the gallery and asked how I might show my work. The people at the gallery suggested, perhaps without much enthusiasm, that I bring in some photos and they would decide if they were interested. I brought in a portfolio and they immediately asked how soon I could exhibit. I said I was retiring in February, so how about May? In addition to exhibiting in the Bay Area, I've exhibited in China and England. I had shows in Leshan and Sichuan, China, in 1989. In 1993, I was recognized as a Fellow at the Royal Photography Society of Great Britain. Seven judges evaluated my portfolio before granting me that honor.

In addition to doing the traditional black and white gelatin silver prints and color prints, I like to experiment and use special and different techniques; I've made solarized photograms as well as infrared and platinum prints. I developed a Polaroid emulsion transfer technique and taught it at the Pacific Art School. For many years, I was a photographer for the Sierra Club. I belong to two camera clubs where I get to meet and talk with other photographers. In the past few years, I've taken courses in digital imaging and I've recently started using a digital camera, although I continue to use my film cameras, as I feel I have more control with film. There is so much to learn; you cannot learn it all in a lifetime. I absorb what I can and have a lot of fun doing it.

I find inspiration in the natural landscape of the Bay Area. I do realistic as well as abstract studies of nature and found objects. I like to take simple objects and see them in a new light. Photography forces you to look, you see more than the average person, you become sensitive to things around you. An everyday object, such as a rag or a garbage can top, can become a piece of art when you pay attention to the play of light and shadow, color contrast and patterns.

Besides photography, I exercise daily, as I think it is important to keep body and mind active. I do Luk Tung Kuen with a large group every morning from 8-9 a.m. at the San Mateo Central Park. I've been doing this for the past eleven years. As I've gotten older, my balance doing the exercises is not as good as it used to be. But I do the best I can. Every Wednesday, I go on a hike with the Sierra Club and we usually average eight miles. We do this rain or shine and it is like a religion to me. I have my share of aches and pains and have a chronic back problem. I'm not a perfect specimen but I do pretty well for a man who will be ninety this December.

San Mateo, California

John Chan and his wife, Cecelia, and their two daughters moved from San Francisco to San Mateo in 1951. John and Cecelia have lived in the same house since then. Cecelia worked in a sewing factory and at the San Mateo Farmer's Market until her retirement. Both daughters and their families live in the Bay Area. One daughter teaches elementary school and the other daughter trains dental technicians. The Chans are proud of the academic and career achievements of their daughters and two granddaughters. John enjoys spending time with family and friends, he gardens and he still does maintenance work on his house.

Albine Bech
Age 79
Tai Chi and Aquatic Exercise Teacher
Elementary School Tutor

This is a big year for me—I'll be eighty in May. I had no idea what I was going to do when I retired at age seventy-two, eight years ago. Things just came my way and I've been able to do the things I've wanted.

I was born in Madagascar in 1925. My parents were French and had moved to Madagascar when they were newly married. My family moved back to France in 1931 when I was six years old. My mother wanted to go back because there were no good schools in the village for my younger brother and me. She was also lonely as there were no European women in the area. We moved around a lot in France. We first stayed with relatives in Paris and then moved on to Toulouse and later to Marseilles. In 1939, my father was called up to serve in the French Army and as a result he lost a very good job, and we lost the comfortable lifestyle my parents had finally attained. We suffered the hardships of war and then suffered through the German occupation and the scarcity of food.

When I was a young girl in France I wanted to be a physical education teacher; however, when the war came I couldn't get the necessary education. My parents were afraid of what was coming. They wanted to be sure I could support myself if something happened to them, so they put me in a college to learn office work. In addition, because of the war, I had to give up studying the violin, which I had studied for ten years.

After liberation, I took an office job with the American Army. The job allowed me to bring home strange food like cornflakes and spam and luxuries like chocolate and soap. It was heaven. I met my future husband, Marvin, an American G.I., through my job. I followed him to the U.S. and had the adventure of being on a war bride ship with 400 brides from 20 countries. The small town in Iowa, where my husband and his family lived, was a culture shock and I felt like an alien. Marvin agreed to leave Iowa after his chicken business failed. The years that followed were hectic as we had three young children and made numerous moves in the U.S., Germany and France. We divorced after twelve years of marriage and I fought for and won custody of our three children. The divorce may have alienated my eldest son, Dan, who later cut himself off from me, as well as from his younger brother and sister.

I had a good job in France as a translator for the American Army but I lost the job in 1967 when the American Army bases closed. It became a struggle to earn a decent living and raise my children as a single parent. A friend from California, whom I had met in France, helped me to come back to the U.S. in 1970. I fell in love with Northern California and decided to make it my permanent home. My youngest son, Terry, came over with me and my daughter, Kildine, came a year later. I initially had a very hard time as I couldn't find a job and had trouble getting credit.

During my lifetime I've worked as a secretary, as a translator, as an interpreter-secretary and in the U.S. as an administrative assistant at Stanford Research and the Syntex Corporation. After I lost vision in one eye at the age of fifty, I looked for different employment and got a job as a salesperson in a shop. I worked in a number of different stores, primarily selling dresses. My last job before I retired was at the East-West bookstore.

I've always loved exercise, which I did practice more or less all my life. I'm in good health and don't take any medicines. Fifteen years ago I took a Tai Chi class and became good at that, and the instructor asked me to start teaching some of the classes. That got me started and I found out then that I am good at teaching. I've always loved swimming and I joined an aquatic exercise group after I retired. The instructor saw I had a talent for it and she asked me to substitute teach for her. I teach her class two or three times a month and during her annual vacations. I've been doing this for about six years; it is very rewarding and I also get paid, which is nice.

I've been involved in two other teaching projects. I've been trained to teach seniors how to use a new technology—Web-TV. It is a way to access the Internet and send and receive e-mails using TV. I had eight students and I loved doing it and had very good results. In the past four years, I've participated in a Rotary Club project tutoring Mexican children in a Redwood City public elementary school. I'm presently tutoring a little girl every week. With all these projects my desire to teach has finally been realized.

In 1980 I decided to pursue a spiritual path and studied the works of Yogananda, who became my guru. I started meditating, doing yoga and became a vegetarian. Meditation has changed my life. I meditate an hour every day. It centers me and helps me live in the moment. I forget my body, and I am one with the cosmic consciousness, or God, or whatever one wants to call it. Meditation also helps me maintain perspective so little things don't bother me. I've gone on a number of silent retreats and found the silence and meditation very cleansing for mind and spirit. Some of the Jesuit Center retreats I've attended combine Christian and Zen paths.

I've had to cope with a lot of things in my life—losses, disappointments and struggles. But now I have a great life and my children have good lives. And I love what I am doing.

Palo Alto, California

Albine Bech lives in a studio apartment in Lytton Gardens in Palo Alto. Her son, Terry, and daughter, Kildine, and their families live in the Bay Area, not too far from her. Albine has five grandchildren and one great-grandchild. She is looking forward to her eightieth birthday celebration with her family and large circle of friends. She has written a memoir of her life, which she has shared with her family.

Sheldon Markel
Age 70
Artist

Let me start at the "real" beginning. When I was a kid I used to draw a lot and people noticed. My mother told me that when I was in elementary school, I was invited, based on the recommendation of the school, to be in a special program at the Detroit Institute of Art. But my parents never sent me. I forgot about art, didn't do any artwork from about age eight or ten until twelve years ago, when I was fifty-eight years old.

I grew up in Detroit and was the second of three children and the only boy. My father was an immigrant from Poland who worked in the men's clothing business; my mother was from Western Canada. My father died of a heart attack when I was fifteen and I needed to work throughout high school and while I was in college.

When I was in school, I thought I would like to be an architect but I gave up on that idea when I didn't do well in math. I went to Wayne State University in Detroit for two years and then to the University of Michigan. I was about to go to Dental School but then decided against it at the last minute, and eventually, after taking more undergraduate courses, got into the University of Michigan's Medical School. I had an internship at the U.S. Public Health Service Hospital on Staten Island, came back to Michigan for a residency in pathology at the University of Michigan, served as a pathologist in the army for two years and then was offered a job in the Pathology Department at St. Joseph Hospital.

I worked at St. Joe's for thirty-two years. Initially, my primary interest was in surgical pathology. Over the course of my career, the emphasis changed. I hadn't anticipated being a department head but was elected to that position by my colleagues for eighteen straight years. While department head, I became involved in the development and implementation of better delivery systems, systems that are now used by many departments of pathology. I retired in 2000 at age sixty-five.

I was always interested in art and my wife, Geri, and I started collecting art the first year of our marriage. In fact, our house was designed with places to exhibit our art collection. I always thought that when I retired I would study art history. At a much later time I started thinking, "Wait a minute, I don't have to make a living out of it, so instead of doing art history, why not do art?"

Twelve years ago, my wife drew my attention to a course on drawing on the right side of the brain (i.e., a technique that enables students to shift to the artist's right-hemisphere mode of seeing—intuitive, insightful, emotional, rather than using the left-hemisphere mode—analytic, objective, linear), and she suggested we take the course together. The course was the beginning and I just took off from there and was drawing all the time.

That went on for about two years and then one day Geri came home and said she had a present for me: she had found a person who she thought would be a great art teacher for me—Julie Bedore, a local artist. So I took my portfolio to Julie and she cut a deal with me; she would take me on if I did the homework and did exactly what she told me to do. I later learned that she thought I was doing good illustrations (very precise and tight) but not art. I accepted her "deal" and so we started. I was initially working in charcoal and after a while she said, "You can draw most anything so let's try some color," and I started painting. A number of months later Julie said, "You are ready," and she encouraged me to show my work to a gallery owner. That led to my first exhibit in 1998. In retrospect, the pieces weren't all that great; I'm a lot better now, although I did sell a lot at that first exhibit. Other exhibits followed and I have been in a number of juried shows. I was having my work framed at the Pierre Paul Gallery and the owner invited me to show my paintings. Since then I have been exhibiting there and the gallery has been handling the sale of my work.

In the past two years, I've been going to a workshop in the fall and spring with Leslie Masters; there are usually about eight of us, all selling artists. She walks around and gives us comments as we work and at the end of the day we critique each other's work. I think I have had a breakthrough due to Leslie's encouragement. My work has become looser, more powerful, more integrated; it is less a color drawing and more a painting.

I paint primarily in acrylics and, while I really like to paint living things like people and horses, I mostly paint still life because I can do that anytime of day or night. Art has become such an important part of my life; it is a blessing to be able to do it. I get such a high out of the creative process. I also get a high when my work sells though it is important to paint what I want and not what I think will sell.

There must be some talent for art in my family. My mother could draw and one of my sisters went to art school and became an art teacher. And I have a daughter who went to the Rhode Island School of Design.

For about seven years I was both practicing medicine and painting. My retirement was planned. I liked what I was doing but it was getting harder to do. I sensed I wasn't able to concentrate as intensely and I didn't feel like reading journals every night to keep up. There were other things I wanted to do.

In addition to painting, I presently work about ten hours a week as the Executive Director of the Huron Valley Physicians Association. I was involved in starting the organization twenty-five years ago. The association represents about eight hundred local private-practice physicians in contract negotiations and problem solving with managed-care organizations.

My wife, Geri, is an educational psychologist who presently works as a private consultant. We have three children; I still say that although our son died almost a year ago. He had been in a bad skiing accident a year before his death. He seemed to be healthy and then died in his sleep. I used to say I was dealt a great hand in life and had everything. Then all of a sudden, life changed overnight. The good thing is that my son and I had no unresolved issues between us. Since his death I have driven myself to be more expressive in my art.

I've been in good health. I did have an angioplasty a few weeks after I retired and have been doing well with it. I pay attention to what I eat, stay physically active and play tennis and golf.

Rabbi Goldstein of the Chabad House contacted me a number of years ago and I started meeting with him on a regular basis. I've been learning Hebrew over the past three or four years and I find Orthodox services, which I attend, to be especially involving. I don't consider myself to be very observant but I do now pay more attention to the Sabbath and I've become very aware of my Judaism. I don't know if I am a person of faith but I do find the rituals and involvement in a religious community to be of increasing importance to me.

Ann Arbor, Michigan

Sheldon Markel (b. 1935) and his wife, Geraldine, have been married for forty-five years. Their family, which includes seven grandchildren, all live in the Ann Arbor area.

Tyrone (Super T) Smith
Age 63
Leader and Vocalist for the Tyrone Smith Revue
Middle School Basketball Team Coach

Music has been the thread running through my life. My mother was a musician who played the piano in church. My father, a Methodist minister, was in a quartet that sang spirituals. My two sisters are musicians, one is a pianist and the other is a vocalist.

I grew up in Memphis and I started singing and dancing in clubs in Arkansas when I was nine or ten years old. We were poor and the money I earned was helpful. I had no formal music training but I had a good ear and picked up music easily. I formed my own band when I was in high school and later joined a band as a vocalist when I moved to Nashville to attend Tennessee State University. I soon realized that I could do a better job than the bandleader and eventually started up my own band. That was back in 1966 and my band has been going ever since.

After I graduated from Tennessee State, I got a job teaching Physical Education in the Nashville Public Schools and taught for thirty-eight years. My band continued to perform throughout most of those years. I would often come off the road after a weekend of performing and go straight to school to teach. I kept up that schedule for twenty-eight years and it is amazing, now that I think about it, that I didn't collapse.

I retired two years ago when I was sixty-one. The school system was offering incentives for early retirement and I had already started thinking that I couldn't keep up the pace at which I was going. Although I loved teaching, I decided to take the opportunity offered. I also knew that I could continue to coach, which was very important to me.

I never devoted much thought to what I would do in retirement, as I already knew I wanted to continue with the music I love. I wanted to expand on it, do bigger things with it. And that's exactly what I have been able to do. In fact, as a result of retiring, I'm working more than I ever did before.

Since my retirement, the band has recorded a CD, *Live with Super T and the Tyrone Smith Revue.* We are presently working on another CD, I haven't decided on the title yet. I have been writing more music and the band is busier than ever. I do a lot of the bookings myself but I also have booking agents all over the country. We are one of the top show and dance bands in the Southeast and we play at colleges, conventions, festivals, proms, bar mitzvahs, weddings, and corporate functions. Recently, we have been booked at more corporate events and wedding receptions; we are playing at least one wedding reception every weekend.

The band plays a wide variety of music since we play for such different audiences. We play classic selections from the '50s, '60s, '70s, Motown, ballads, rhythm and blues, and the latest top 40. I don't write up a song list beforehand; I wait until I "feel" the audience, study them, and then decide what we will play. We don't practice; we don't need to since we perform so often. If we have to learn a new piece, let's say a bride and groom request a particular song to dance to, we usually learn it in the van on the way to the job.

We play long sets. Most bands play a forty-five minute set and then they take a break. We play two straight hours, sometimes as long as three and the audiences prefer it. It separates us from the rest of the bands. When I was a kid, the longer I danced, the more money I made, so I guess I just became used to performing like this.

Many of my band members have been with me a long time—some as long as twenty-three, twenty-two and eighteen years. That's a long time for a band and we have become like a family. The band includes five horn players, two guitarists, two keyboard players and a drummer. Three of the

male musicians are vocalists and sometimes we have a female vocalist, depending on the job. I'm the leader, vocalist and sometimes a percussionist, but I primarily consider myself an entertainer.

The band is known as a high-energy band and I have the reputation for getting the audience involved. Audiences know me as "Super T." My trademark is to begin a show in a tuxedo and change into my costume for the second set. It is a bright blue jumpsuit emblazoned with a large "T," a red cape and red ankle boots. I turn an event into one big party. I like to make people happy and I like them to have a good time. That's my reward.

In December 2003, we were invited to play a Christmas party at the White House. At the party, I invited the President, First Lady and the twins onto the stage. I joked that the Secret Service should stand back as I was taking over. I instructed the First Family to do my "Super T Booty Green Dance." (Put your hands on your knees. Bend over. Shake two times to the right, shake two times to the left.) The First Family got right down and the East Room erupted. I later led a conga line through the formal state rooms on the White House first floor. *USA Today* had an article about it.

I shook the President's hand at the end and jokingly said we would love to play at an inaugural ball if he were reelected. And, to my surprise, we got a call to do just that. We performed at the largest ball, the Texas-Wyoming ball, in January 2005. I consider myself a longtime independent but I was thrilled to be playing at an inauguration, be it for a Republican or Democrat.

In addition to the band, I coach a Middle School basketball team. Although I like the team to win tournaments, I see my role as being more than a coach. I understand the disadvantaged backgrounds the kids come from, as it is not so dissimilar from my own. I grew up near the projects in Memphis and we were surrounded by poverty and broken homes and I witnessed some terrible things. I don't know how my parents managed raising five kids in that atmosphere and on their limited income.

I try to teach the team members self-discipline and responsibility, as well as instill self-confidence and a belief in their abilities. I insist they do their homework, I check their grades and I don't let them practice or play if their homework isn't complete and if they don't maintain a certain grade point average. I often meet former students who tell me how I helped them and how I made a difference in their lives. It is so gratifying to me to see these kids go on to college and have careers.

My religious faith is important to me. I am a member of the Baptist Capitol Hill Church in Nashville, although I rarely attend services because I am on the road so much. I feel that God has blessed me and given me a good life. I have a wonderful wife who puts up with me, understands me and supports what I do. Helen, my wife, and I have been together a long time. We started dating in high school, continued dating at Tennessee State, and have now been married for thirty-nine years. Helen is employed as a schoolteacher in the Nashville school system. We have one daughter, Prudence, the light of my life, who is an attorney and lives in Houston. I'd say that my family and the band members, who are like a second family, are the significant relationships in my life. I really don't have time for other relationships. I'm also blessed to be healthy; performing and dancing on stage gives me a workout and keeps me fit.

My life has been very fulfilling and things keep getting better. I hope to be doing exactly what I am doing now in ten years, when I am seventy-three. And ten years from then, when I'm eighty-three, I hope to still be doing the same thing. There is, however, one thing I haven't yet accomplished. I would love to have one hit record. That's my goal; that's what I'm working towards.

Nashville, Tennessee

––––––––––––

Author's Note: I heard about Tyrone from a friend in Nashville who facilitated my contact with him. I had not previously known about "Super T" but he is clearly well known in certain entertainment circles, particularly in the south. Tyrone suggested that we meet for our interview at the downtown Nashville Hilton Hotel. He was performing for a business convention at the hotel that evening and wanted to take care of some last-minute arrangements. We agreed to meet in the lobby and when asked how I might recognize him, he described himself as a short black man with an Afro. As we walked through the lobby after the interview, a number of people in business suits who were attending the convention recognized him and approached him, saying, "I'm looking forward to the performance tonight Super T." I was looking forward to it as well since he had graciously invited me and a companion to be his guests that evening.

He has frequently been described in reviews as an amazing, ageless, dynamic showman, whose band sets the standard for high-energy shows. And I can certainly attest to that. He quickly got the audience involved and turned the event into a big, happy party. My only regret was that I had to leave at the end of the first set. My son, who had accompanied me, had to get to work early the next morning, so I missed seeing Tyrone come out in his "Super T" costume in the second set.

Dean Bush
Age 77
Maker of Musical Instruments
Woodworker
Antique Shop Owner

I've always had a workshop and my present workshop is my favorite place to be. I've been doing woodworking since I was in high school where I specialized in industrial arts. I've had many different careers but woodworking and building things have always been part of my life. Retirement freed me so that I have more time to make and repair instruments and to build and restore furniture. In addition, retirement allowed me to set up my antique shop.

I grew up in a small community in Cannon County, Tennessee. After high school I attended a business school in Nashville and that is where I met my wife, Jean. She has been my partner for fifty-six years. We settled in Waverly, Tennessee, where Jean's family lived. Waverly presently has a population of about 5,000 residents.

Jean's father helped me land my first job, which was as a photographer at the Tennessee Valley Authority plant in Johnsonville. I had learned photography skills when I served in the Marine Corps during the Korean conflict. I was sent to Parris Island rather than Korea, and once they found out I was handy with a camera, they put me to work in the photography lab. I stayed with the TVA as an industrial photographer for ten years. During that time I also built a hunting and fishing lodge from scratch and operated it for a while.

A lawyer friend and I decided that a radio station would be a great thing to have in this community and we submitted an application for a permit to the Federal Communications Commission. We didn't get the permit but a man named Bob McKay, who was already in the radio business, got it instead. McKay offered me the job as station manager and I accepted it. WPHC (it later became WPHC/WVRY) went on the air in September 1963. I stayed with the station for twenty years.

A memorable experience while I was station manager was the 1978 explosion of liquid propane gas in Waverly. Twenty-three cars of a freight train derailed in a populated area and two of the derailed tankers contained 22,000 gallons each of liquid propane gas. I had been on the scene, twenty feet from the tankers, interviewing the police chief while we waited for the trucks to come and transfer the gas from the railroad cars. The police chief wanted evacuation procedures broadcast on the radio so I went back to the station to put the information on the air. I had been gone four or five minutes when one of the tankers exploded. I had missed being killed by just a few minutes.

Five people, including the police chief, were instantly killed and sixteen people eventually died of injuries. It was a terrible tragedy for the community. Our station went into emergency broadcast status and remained on the air for thirty-six consecutive hours. We were the only link to the general public and handled over 1,800 phone calls. WPHC/WVRY won many awards for the public service we had performed and Senator Jim Sasser recorded the station's contributions in the Congressional Record.

I next went into the cable TV business. We were in a fringe TV area in Waverly as the nearest station was sixty-five miles away in Nashville. We applied and got a franchise to build a cable system here, formed a corporation, and sold stocks—and the cable service we developed worked well. A party from New York purchased our cable business nine years later. I then retired for the first time at age fifty-five. I didn't stay retired for long and went to work for the gas company. While I was there I did their design work and mapped their system. Over the years, while I was pursuing these different careers, I also did work as a commercial photographer, was a stringer for a CBS affiliate and the *Nashville Tennessean*, and owned a dry

cleaning business. I had to retire from the gas company at age sixty-five and that brings me up to my "real retirement."

Once I retired I turned my attention to instrument making, woodworking and setting up an antique shop. I got into instrument making because I wanted to learn how to play the fiddle. My brother, who passed away three years ago, was a professional musician who recorded country and western music. He wouldn't give me one of his fiddles and I didn't want to pay for an expensive violin that I didn't know how to play. So I decided to build one for myself and that's how I got started.

The first one I made wasn't particularly good and I made many mistakes. Since then I've done a lot of research on the history and construction of violins and my violins have gotten better over time. Violins must be made out of certain wood; the back has to be hard maple and the top must be soft spruce. Initially, I had the local lumber company order wood for me. Now I order from the International Violin Company in Baltimore. They provide me with wood from Germany as the German maple is harder and the spruce softer than the wood grown here. The age and quality of the wood affects the tone of the instrument but I find chance plays a role as well. I'm told that musicians in Branson, Missouri, are using at least two of my fiddles. Sometimes my fiddles come back to me for repair from people I didn't sell them to. Although I've learned to make the instrument, I never could learn to play it.

The two other instruments I build are dulcimers and steel guitars. The first dulcimer I built was from a kit. I then gave the kit away and now I design my dulcimers and make them larger so they have more volume. I do a lot of repair work on mandolins and guitars but I don't build them. I also love to work on repairing old pump organs as the engineering fascinates me. I had to order books on how they work before I could start repairing them.

I've also built a lot of furniture for the public; the popular things I've built are benches, lawn furniture, harvest tables and cabinets. I also refinish and repair furniture and restore antiques. I have an advantage over other antique dealers, as they tend not to bid at auctions on antiques that are broken. As a result, I am able to get them cheaper and then fix them in my workshop.

When Jean's parents passed away we acquired buildings they had owned. They had lived in one building, run a restaurant in another, and a store in a third building. We started off slowly with one building and now we have four buildings. One building is for my workshop, two are showrooms and one is for storage. I'm either at my workshop or the showrooms from nine to five every weekday. Tourists coming through town are my biggest customers.

I'm involved in the community in many ways. My big community project at the present time is being chairman of the Music on the Square committee. Music on the Square is a city project that started in 2001. Every Saturday night from June through August we put on a three-hour music show. We invite musicians from Nashville to come and perform. A former resident underwrites the musicians so that the performances are free. In addition to the music, we have booths sponsored by non-profit organizations. We provide quality entertainment and good food and people have a lot of fun. In addition to being chairman of the committee, I also serve as Master of Ceremonies and take care of the sound system. We have between 1,500 and 3,000 people attending every Saturday night. It creates quite a bit of interest for a town this small. I'm also a member of the city's finance committee and past president of the Rotary Club.

Our social life is primarily through our church, the Waverly Church of Christ. I was reared in the church and I'd say that religion is number one in my life. I've been a deacon for thirty years. We go to church every Sunday, Sunday night and Wednesday night.

I've had a few medical problems but I'm now in good health; I don't smoke or drink and I eat good food. I get a lot of exercise and also put in a lot of time working on our garden and orchard.

We've had a very good life living here in our small town.

Waverly, Tennessee

Dean Bush (b. 1929) and his wife have one daughter, two sons and five grand-children. Their daughter is Executive Director of United Cerebral Palsy of Middle Tennessee and President of the League of Women Voters of Nashville. Their older son is Director of the Indiana Dental Association and lives in Indianapolis. Their younger son is a minister in Evansville, Indiana.

Carrie Lo
Age 74
Artist
Arts and Crafts Teacher

I was born in Shanghai, China; my father was Filipino and my mother was Chinese. When the Communists took over we had to leave and we moved to the Philippines. I always loved to draw as a child and when I was a young student in Shanghai, my paintings were placed on the bulletin board to be shown to the school. This piqued my interest and encouraged me to take up painting. Art became a hobby.

My husband and I married in the Philippines and he didn't want me to continue working when I was pregnant with our first child (it was easy to be an obedient wife about that). During my pregnancy, I studied Chinese brush painting and calligraphy with Professor Chan Bing Sun. I enjoyed it very much and it resulted in a teacher-student show at the China Art Gallery in the Philippines. After my first child was born, I became involved in childcare and domestic responsibilities and didn't do much artwork. I might periodically do a little and then I'd let it go.

My husband, who was Chinese, was granted a pre-arranged-employment visa that allowed him to work in the Philippines. He was supposed to return to Hong Kong when it expired, which we didn't want to do. He was employed as a chemist and he had contacts in both Germany and the States. He asked me which country I would prefer and I chose the United States, as I was fluent in English. I have never regretted that decision and my children all benefited from it. In 1969, when I was thirty-seven years old, we immigrated to the United States and settled in New York City. My

105

time was taken up raising our three children and managing a household. My children grew up, went away to college and then my husband got sick. He had cancer of the liver. We tried everything here and went to China for four months where he had family. We believed that Chinese herbal treatment would help but in the end, it didn't. It was very, very difficult for me when I lost him. We had a good marriage and I loved him very much. My children were all grown and the two older ones were married. It really was an empty nest. My youngest son stayed with me for a while. That was sixteen years ago and I still get teary talking about it. After my husband passed away, to ease my grief and as a form of therapy, I took up watercolor painting.

I started studying watercolor painting with Denis Ponsot at the Craft Student League. He is an excellent teacher and he was very encouraging. I went wherever he was teaching in order to take courses with him. In addition to studying with Denis Ponsot, I later took art classes at the Art Student League, the Brooklyn Botanical Gardens, and the 92nd St. "Y." I didn't want to go back to Chinese brush painting, which I found confining and subdued. It is also very demanding and difficult; if you make one mistake the painting is gone. I found watercolor to be the closest thing to Chinese art. I also found it to be vibrant, colorful and free. I love the medium and have been painting in it ever since. For a while, in response to the encouragement of a good friend, I tried using oil paints and pastels; but I didn't like working with them and went back to my first love, watercolor.

Painting brings me joy and it is very therapeutic. When I'm painting, I concentrate exclusively on the work; I forget all my troubles and the things that bother me. It got me through the very difficult time after my husband died and it is still very therapeutic for me.

I love the beauty of nature and it is the source of my inspiration. Flowers and landscapes are my favorite subjects. The artists whose work I admire the most are John Singer Sargent, Winslow Homer, Georgia O'Keefe, and my teacher, Denis Ponsot. They inspire me with their use of color and technique. I think my paintings merge Eastern and Western influences.

They are also a mix of realism and impressionism depending on my interpretation of the object I'm painting, and how it speaks to me.

I had worked as an executive secretary and administrator for China Airlines for many years and retired at age sixty-five. Retirement allowed me to devote more time to art and eventually, through the encouragement of my teacher, fellow students and friends, I started to exhibit my paintings in various locations. I joined two associations, the prestigious Pen and Brush (an association of women painters, sculptors and writers) and the West Side Arts Coalition (a group of painters, photographers and sculptors). Membership in these associations gives me the opportunity to exhibit my paintings in group shows. In addition to sales at exhibits, my work is sold on the Internet. I joined the Internet art world in 2000 and my paintings are now on a website.

Three years ago I fell and broke my elbow. As soon as I fell I thought, and remember saying to my son, "My painting career is over." I had an elbow replacement and I have persevered. I no longer can do the detail work I used to do on flowers. I'm doing more landscapes, which don't involve as much detail. My flowers are now freer; in fact all my work is freer. I've become more courageous and experimental and I try new things. Painting is a constant learning process for me. It is always a challenge and I love it that way.

Along the way, I picked up crafts as a hobby. I make various greeting cards, sew tote bags and pillowcases and make jewelry. I particularly like making pendants, necklaces, and earrings. I'm also teaching for Elder Craftsmen, an organization in New York City that helps seniors be more creative. It came about this way. I was taking an art class at the "Y" and joined an exercise class at the nearby Lenox Hill Neighborhood House. I met this lady who volunteers for Elder Craftsmen at the exercise class. She found out that I painted and she mentioned that they were looking for someone with a painting background to teach seniors. Some of my paintings were on the wall from the art class and I flippantly said, "You can look at my paintings and see if you like them." Her employer did check them out and liked what she saw and contacted me right away. She invited me to join their organization and become a teacher. I wasn't sure I was qualified but she assured me that I was. So they have been sending me out to different senior centers around the city to teach arts and crafts courses. My first assignment was in Harlem. It has been a rich experience for me to help people be creative and bring joy into their lives. I think when you give, you receive back many times over. It is a blessing to be able to give. I speak a number of languages, including numerous Chinese dialects, which is an advantage when I teach at some of the centers.

I'm fortunate that my three children, their spouses and my three grandchildren all live in the city. I have a large circle of friends and meet with them often. I have a group of friends from New Jersey, where I lived for ten years, and we get together regularly for karaoke and chorale singing. I make friends easily and I keep my friends; I was an only child so friendships were always important to me. I still keep in contact with childhood and high school friends and visit them in California and Canada.

I keep very busy and I am seldom idle. I go to an exercise program twice a week, which includes forty-five minutes of aerobics, stretching and weights. In addition, I go line-dancing once a week. I used to do ballroom dancing but since I broke my elbow I have difficulty in twirling and turning, so I gave it up. Like most New Yorkers, I don't have a car and I walk a lot in the city. Keeping myself mentally as well as physically fit is important; I read, work on crossword puzzles and computer games. I continue to take painting classes; it ensures that I have weekly studio time. I would love to have a solo show someday. That's a goal of mine.

New York City

––––––––––––

Carrie Lo (b. 1932) lives in an apartment in Manhattan. The following was written about her work in a review of a West Side Arts Coalition group show in the publication Gallery & Studio. *Lo has "…combined linear grace of Chinese ink painting with more intense Western-style color areas in a lively group of watercolors. Lo's close-up composition of sensual pink flowers contrasted dramatically with a picture of two small children romping in a meadow. Both, however, possessed a lovely lyricism."* *Ms. Lo's paintings are in collections in Taiwan, Canada and the United States.*

David Herzig
Age 69
Woodworker
Pharmaceutical Industry Consultant

"Retirement" is a word I dislike intensely and do not use. What people refer to as retirement has for me been a time to change careers and focus. I worked for Parke-Davis, a division of Warner-Lambert Pharmaceutical Company, for thirty-one years and was Vice President for Drug and Scientific Development when I left in 1999, at age sixty-two. Since then, I've been dividing my time, almost equally, between consulting, keeping up with science, and with woodworking. I consult on a selective basis on drug development, biotechs and start-ups and I stay involved in science by going to national meetings and reading a good selection of journals. I'm presently spending between thirty to forty percent of my time woodworking.

I've been playing with woodworking most of my life. My father, who was a dentist, used to do a lot of stuff around the house. I started working with him when I was a kid, as early as age six, seven or eight. We built what became the family room in the basement, putting in paneling and a staircase. I've always done work around the house. When my children were young and needed desks, I'd put together something simple for them. My professional career involved long-term projects, and at the end of a busy day I might have a couple of pieces of paper and another to-do list to show for it. So it was nice to be able to come home and work on something that gave me immediate, tangible results.

I knew I wanted to do woodworking when I left Warner-Lambert. I also knew that I wanted to "do it right" and get good training, so I went to the Mark Adams School of Woodworking in Indianapolis. The school brings in

111

some of the best woodworkers around the country and they give courses in different aspects of woodworking. I've been there about five times, for a week each time. I selected courses on the basis of who was teaching and what I wanted to learn. I eventually set up a shop in my basement and started challenging myself to see if I could do more and more different and increasingly difficult things. Except in one case, I've never done the same piece twice. Each piece has to present a different challenge. I primarily make cabinets and tables. Most of my work has been done for family members but other people have now started commissioning pieces.

Woodworking is both gratifying and frustrating for me. Frustrating because it doesn't always come out the way I want. I'm always making mistakes; hopefully I don't make the same ones twice. But one of the beauties of woodworking is that you can correct errors. It can be a challenge to take a mistake and turn it into a design feature. I am mastering the *craft* of furniture making, my skills have improved over time and I probably can make anything that I look at. That is the gratifying part. But I don't know if I have the talent for the *art* of woodworking, for creating new designs. I would like to have it and it frustrates me because I don't know yet if I do.

I received a Ph.D. in Organic Chemistry from the University of Cincinnati and before my job at Parke-Davis, I worked at NIH and N.Y.U. Medical School. Science was the core of my work at Parke-Davis although I needed to get involved in acquisitions, licensing, patents, manufacturing and marketing. I had many exciting times developing and bringing new drugs to market but at some point, around age sixty-one, it dawned on me that it was no longer as much fun. I realized I had already answered variations of the same questions I was being asked. I felt it was time to move on. You come to the realization that there are other things to learn in life. According to company policy, I could retire at age sixty-two without penalty, and I did.

Last year I took Law School classes on-line. I wanted the intellectual challenge of something I'd never done before. Studying law has similarities to studying Talmud; both involve trying to understand the reasoning or logic in an argument and how to go about constructing a logical argument. I stopped taking courses after one year because I missed the dialogue, the intellectual exchange that occurs in a classroom. I may try to sit in on courses at the Law School here.

My health is good and I recently ran in a marathon. I used to compete in fencing on an international level and ran five miles a day as part of my training. I stopped fencing but continue to run, as it has been a good way to stay fit. I probably made seventy-five or eighty trips to Europe and Japan when I worked for Warner-Lambert and I would run early in the mornings. It was lovely running through the empty streets of foreign cities before the workday started there.

My paternal grandfather set a model of achievement for the family. On his own, at the age of thirteen, he left the small Polish village that was his home and eventually immigrated to the United States. Though lacking in formal education, he was fluent in four languages, was learned, and could debate Talmud with rabbis. He became the wholesale distributor for Land O'Lakes Butter and Eggs in Cleveland, started a loan society and was a founder of his synagogue. He and my grandmother supported their two sons through college and dental school. My father followed in his footsteps and was very involved in community service. That's the background I come from and I've tried to live up to it.

My community activities include being on the Board of Directors of the Jewish Federation and of my synagogue. My wife, Phyllis, and I have been sponsors of the University of Michigan's Musical Society. Recently, we joined the founding benefactors of the new UMS Theater Fund. After seeing a compelling production of the Royal Shakespeare Company sponsored by the UMS, we decided to play a role in developing a world-class theater program here. Theater has enhanced our lives and we want to play a role in enabling others to enjoy good theater. We want to contribute and give back to our community.

Ann Arbor, Michigan

David Herzig (b. 1936) and his wife, Phyllis, a social worker, have been married for forty-three years. They have four children and five grandchildren. In addition to the above-mentioned activities, David enjoys time with his family, traveling and gardening.

Laurie (Lawrence) Naiman
Age 73
Photographer
Web Site Designer

"To me, photography is a wonderful tool for discovering the visual magic of the world around me. I'm attracted by ordinary subjects from which I might create something interesting—to evoke an emotional or reflective response in the viewer. Sometimes the results are visually pleasing but not always."
From Laurie Naiman's Palo Alto Camera Club Web Gallery

I would say that since I retired, photography is about sixty percent of my life. I've been taking pictures for over fifty-five years but the nature and quality of my work underwent a major change ten or fifteen years ago. I've been able to nurture that change in retirement.

I became interested in photography as a teenager. My older brother had a passing interest in photography and influenced me. I built my first darkroom in our basement at age fifteen. While in high school, I had a part-time job with a commercial photographer; I assisted him at weddings, in the darkroom, in the mounting area, and I learned quite a bit.

I built my second darkroom at age thirty after I finished my postgraduate training in pediatric hematology. At that time, my first wife and I and our three sons were living in Philadelphia. I was then on the medical faculty at Temple University where I was in charge of the Department of Pediatric Hematology as well as head of hematology at St. Christopher's Children's Hospital. My sons were my primary photography subjects but I also used my photographic skills to take pictures of patients and I learned to take color slides of blood cells under the microscope. The slides were very useful for teaching and publication purposes. Among my publications was a book I co-authored entitled *Hematological Problems of the Newborn*. I stayed at Temple University for twenty years. During that time, I took care of children with serious blood diseases and cancer. When I first started, the chance of a child being cured of leukemia was 2-3% and now it's 70-80%. The major breakthroughs took place in the early 1970s.

In 1984, my second wife and I, with our young daughter, moved to Northern California. I accepted a position as director of the blood bank for the American Red Cross and taught at Stanford's Children's Hospital one day a week. I built another darkroom in our house in Palo Alto and started doing work in color in addition to black and white. A big change took place in my photography when I joined the Palo Alto Camera Club in 1991 or '92. Up until then I was primarily doing family and travel photos. At the club, I began to see other people's work and get feedback on mine. I was encouraged to go beyond the usual documentary stuff that we all do. I was able to talk about photography with friends at the club and I also began to visit museums and galleries to look at photographs.

All of this inspired me to do things differently, to capture the familiar in a different way. I began to look at familiar scenes and see if I could present them differently, such as by moving in closer to a subject or using a different angle or different lighting. I receive a lot of enjoyment out of creating photos that are both interesting to me and interesting to others. I've lost the desire to make photos that appeal to everyone. I derive a great deal of pleasure from the entire photographic process; from the way I see and capture the image in the camera, to what I do with the photo at the computer, to the final image.

I retired on December 31, 1999 at age sixty-seven. My hearing started to fail ten years ago and I had trouble at conferences and lectures. It was one of the reasons why I retired when I did. I had a cochlear implant last year and that has helped. At the same time that I retired, I started developing some web sites. One was for the Red Cross, to publicize the work of the blood program, and the other was a personal one, for family. I became seriously involved in web site design and was asked to design a site for the California Blood Bank Society. I kept that up from 1999 until recently. I also designed a web site for the Palo Alto Camera Club that has information about the club as well as the winning images from the club's competitions. The web site was very instrumental in reviving the camera club. I was president of the club for two or three years. I'm now getting ready to do my own photography web site.

I switched to digital about four years ago and I've just gotten my fifth digital camera. Digital photography requires constant learning. It never stops. Since retirement, I have been able to visit galleries and exhibits at least once a month with friends. My brother told me that one of the worst things about getting old is seeing family and friends get sick and die. I've been learning that lesson as good friends from the camera club have died or become seriously ill.

I'm fortunate I have no serious medical problems. I watch my diet and exercise by walking seven to ten miles a week with our dog. In retirement, I'm able to do all the things I enjoy. I devote a small amount of my time to the practice of medicine and regularly go on pediatric rounds. I have more time for photography, for visits to exhibits and galleries, for work on web sites and camera club activities. I do the shopping and cooking in our house and have time for family and socializing with friends. I enjoy everything I'm doing and I like the balance I've been able to achieve.

Palo Alto, California

Laurie Naiman (b. 1932) a native of Toronto, Canada, graduated from the University of Toronto's Medical School. He has three sons, one daughter, and one grandchild. One of his sons is a professional Fine Arts photographer. His wife, Judy Palmer, is a retired physician who specialized in pediatric pulmonary diseases. She is presently doing an independent research project on the history of women in Death Valley. Laurie sells his photographs and has won first place in a number of photography competitions.

Lois Kivi Nochman
Age 81
World Class Master Swimmer

I started swimming competitively in 1988 at the age of 64. This is the way it came about. I was swimming laps at the local YMCA pool (I always liked to swim and it is the only exercise I enjoy) and another swimmer asked if I would like to swim competitively for the "Y" team. I told her I wasn't particularly interested as it seemed silly to me at my age; I was still thinking of high school and college athletics. She didn't let it drop and came back and said, "But we need you." This was so flattering as I had been thinking that I wasn't needed anymore. I had retired from Highland Park Community College in 1983 after teaching English there for thirty years, my children were all grown and my husband was happy. Feeling flattered and needed, I went along for the ride and joined the Royal Oak YMCA swim team. I started in the 60-64 age bracket (we swim in five-year age groups) so I was at the end of the age group, which is usually a disadvantage. I started swimming in meets and I was spectacular! In my first year of competition I won the 100-yard butterfly in the YMCA spring nationals.

I had not had a plan for my retirement. I had intended to teach until I was sixty-five but retired earlier at age fifty-nine, due to a stressful work situation. After my first few competitive swimming experiences I decided this is something I could do, I enjoyed doing it, and I liked to win. I switched teams after one year because the "Y" team didn't compete in anything beyond their own nationals. Initially, I hadn't known about Masters Swimming or about other meets. I joined the South Oakland Seals and began to compete in U.S. Masters and eventually in World Masters swimming competitions.

In the course of a year, I usually swim in six local Michigan meets, meets in Ohio and Indianapolis, three major Masters competitions (YMCA, Masters Short Course and Masters Long Course) and the Huntsman World Senior Games in Utah. I try to go to the World Masters competitions, which occur every other year, alternating with the Senior Olympics, which I also try to attend. I take part in postal meets and sometimes in the Canadian Nationals. I've been to the World Masters in Munich, Germany, as well as Riccione, Italy, and Queensland, New Zealand. I'm planning to compete in the World Masters in Stanford, California, this coming August.

The butterfly stroke is my specialty as is the individual medley, which includes the butterfly, backstroke, breaststroke and free style. Two years after I won my first butterfly competition at the "Y" nationals in 1988, I set the national record for my age group in the 400-yard individual medley, and two years after that I won my first world championship for my age group in the 50-meter butterfly. I've won over 1000 medals and set 35 national records and 38 world records in the 70-74, 75-79 and 80-84 age brackets. Last month I won nine first-place medals in the 80-84 age bracket at the Huntsman World Senior Games in St. George, Utah. I'm 81, which I realize is close to the bottom of my age group, but even when I get to the top of this age bracket, I don't see anyone coming up who is better than I am.

I was going to put all my medals into a drawer, which is what most swimmers do, but my husband, Marv, said no. He hung the medals, along with the certificates of national and world records, on the walls of the rear first-floor bedroom of our house. All four walls are now blanketed and there is little space left.

There aren't a lot of ladies my age swimming competitively in Michigan. All my competitors live in warmer climates—Florida, Arizona and California. A swimmer needs a swimming pool and one of my problems in Michigan is not having access to a swimming pool where I can swim laps at a convenient time. At the present time, I practice one hour a day on weekdays, as that is all that is available to me at the local "Y" pool. I don't have a personal coach. The "Y" pool is open on weekends but there are other things I need to do; my husband wants to spend time with me, there are children to visit, friends to see and things to do around the house.

My health has been good. Most swimmers have physical problems, usually shoulder problems, and I had rotator cuff tears that required surgery in 2000. It kept me out of competition for a year. My only other physical problem has been hearing loss, which has been bad. It does tend to isolate one.

I learned to swim as a child at my grandparents' summer cottage on an inland lake. I have always loved water—watching it, moving over it, and being in it. When I was growing up in Ann Arbor in the 1930s and '40s there were no public pools or school pools. Girls were allowed to swim at the University of Michigan Union men's pool for fifteen cents from 8 to 11 a.m. on Saturdays if we entered the building through the side door. Women and girls weren't allowed in the front door then. I went swimming there. Matt Mann, the U of M swimming coach, had a hobby of teaching children to swim and opened the U of M intramural pool on Saturdays for that purpose. My brother, a star high school swimmer, came to his notice and Matt Mann allowed me to join his daughter and a cousin in lap swimming while he taught the children. Occasionally he would comment on our swimming form. I also had the privilege of attending his swimming camp for girls as a junior counselor. When I was in high school and college there were no competitive swimming teams for women. Title IX requiring institutions receiving federal funds to offer equal athletic opportunities for women passed in 1972.

I didn't return to swimming until the 1970s when my teaching and family schedule permitted me two hours a week at the YMCA pool. The techniques had changed considerably since I had learned to do them and I needed to work on learning the new techniques.

I would place swimming as the third priority in my life. My first priority is to try to live the life prescribed by the Baha'i faith and my second priority is my family. I became a Baha'i in 1953. Baha'is I met while I was a university student introduced me to the religion. I initially joined out of intellectual conviction and my spirituality developed over time. The Baha'i faith was founded by Baha'u'llah in Iran in the 19th century. Baha'u'llah is seen as the latest in a line of God's prophets including Moses, Jesus and Muhammad and the idea of progressive revelation is of central significance in the faith. Baha'is believe that all religions have the same spiritual foundations, despite their apparent differences. There are six million Baha'is worldwide and 150,000 in the United States.

My family includes Marvin, my husband of fifty-two years, two daughters, Jean and Joyce, one son, Joseph, two grandsons and four great-grandchildren. My daughters are from my first marriage; I was only nineteen and a sophomore in college when I married and the marriage ended in divorce in 1949. Marvin and I married in 1953; we had met at the University five years prior to our marriage.

The meaning of swimming to me is a complex one. I'm very good at it, I like to do it, it's relaxing and I don't feel good if I don't swim. It's like having any skill. For instance, if you have a good singing voice, it hurts not to sing. It's like that for me with swimming. It's very Zen; I become one with the water. I think that's true of anything you master; you become it.

Huntington Woods, Michigan

Lois Kivi Nochman, the younger of two siblings, was born in Detroit in 1924. Her father's family was from Finland and immigrated to the Upper Peninsula of Michigan to work in the copper mines. Her mother's family was among the early settlers in the state. Lois received both B.A. and M.A. degrees in English Literature from the University of Michigan. Her teaching career spanned thirty-three years. She enjoys travel, which she gets to do when she competes in world competitions, and she is an avid reader.

Marvin Nochman
Age 84
Actor and Director

I was teaching English in high school when the drama teacher in the school, who was also the director and president of the local community theater, drafted me into her company's production of *Cyrano de Bergerac*. Cyrano is a big-cast show and they needed more people. I thought, why not, though I had done no theater work at all, unless you count playing George Washington in the sixth grade. I wasn't even an avid theatergoer at the time. I played a double role in the play, the Old Friar and Cardinal Richelieu, parts with very few lines, but I got hooked on theater and have been hooked ever since.

That was in 1975, when I was fifty-four years old, and I've probably been involved in at least one play, sometimes more, every year for the past thirty years. I apprenticed with the Wayne County Players and attended a number of acting workshops; most helpful was a workshop based on the principles of a book entitled *Audition* written by Michael Shurtleft. Most of my theater work has been with community theaters and the group that I'm now most associated with is the Rosedale Community Players in Detroit. I've also worked with festival companies performing Shakespeare such as the Michigan Shakespeare Festival in Jackson and Shakespeare in the Park in Royal Oak. I've been in some TV commercials, for which I get paid, as well as some locally made low-budget films.

My first major role was in *The Prisoner of Second Avenue*, a play by Neil Simon. It's a tale of a married couple trying to survive in a New York apartment building after the husband loses his job. I've been in quite a few plays by Neil Simon; they are not great plays but they are fun to do. I've played a broad range of roles over the years, from an evil character in *Veronica's Room,* a thriller by Ira Levin, to Shakespeare. I don't have a favorite role; all have been interesting and fun. Bad guys are always more interesting to play than good guys and playing in Shakespeare is always a delight. Roles for old men are hard to come by and fortunately there are plenty of old men in Shakespeare's plays. Some of the roles I've played are the Old Shepherd in *Winter's Tale,* Duncan and Siward in *Macbeth* and Gloucester in *King Lear.*

There used to be a theater festival in Detroit called the Mort Furay Festival, in which local community theater groups would present scenes for adjudication. I always received good marks and was awarded the Best Supporting Actor for a scene in *The Good Doctor* (a Neil Simon play) and Best Actor for a scene in *Veronica's Room.*

I've branched out into directing and I've probably directed about twelve plays. I think the play I most enjoyed directing was *The Lion in Winter,* a play written by James Goldman. The Rosedale Community Players have not only given me awards for acting, they have also acknowledged my directing and have given me trophies for directing at several of their annual awards dinners.

Learning lines has always been difficult and time consuming for me. I don't feel comfortable until I have the lines down cold. Movement on stage and the business of relationships between characters come fairly easy to me. I can also go along easily with changing interpretations or the way a line is presented if a director asks for it.

I have suffered considerable hearing loss and that makes being in theater more difficult. In one of the last plays I was in, I made entrances from way backstage but the cues for the entrances were delivered downstage. I needed someone to assist me with the cues. Not hearing the cues is one of the worst parts of hearing loss. But so far I've been able to manage it.

I still get emotional highs with every production. There is so much ego satisfaction. I'm thinking, "This is my scene, I can do it, and I'm going to make you enjoy it." I'm eighty-four years old and it is a pleasure to work with younger people; it energizes me.

My other major interests are reading, which I have always enjoyed, and playing tennis. In the winter I play once or twice a week and in the summer I play almost daily. My health is pretty good and I try to stay healthy and fit. My wife, Lois, is a wonderful example of health and fitness and she keeps me on my toes.

Lois and I are both Baha'is and the religion is a very meaningful and important part of our lives. Lois was a Baha'i when we married in 1953 and she introduced me to the religion. I declared my commitment to the faith five years after our marriage.

My parents were living in Ypsilanti, Michigan, when I was born. I was the only son and eldest of three. My father owned a men's clothing store and lost everything in the 1929 crash. After that we moved to Detroit to live with extended family. My mother died when I was fourteen. Her death was very difficult for me and I had a hard time psychologically. I was drafted into the army a year after I graduated from high school and I served in the Pacific during World War II. Upon return, the G.I. Bill enabled me to go to the University of Michigan. I was very grateful, as I could not have gone to college without it. I changed my major three times before I decided that I liked English so much that I wanted to spend my life involved in it in some way. The only way I could think of was as a schoolteacher, so I got a teaching certificate in addition to B.A. and M.A. degrees in English Literature.

I couldn't find a teaching job after graduation so I took a job with the Ford Motor Company. I was there for five years when someone told me about a teaching opportunity with the Wayne School District. It involved a considerable cut in pay but I decided that if I were ever going to do it, I had better do it then, before I had too much invested in Ford. I taught high school English for twenty years and retired at age sixty-five. I never regretted my decision.

I think it is important for people my age to keep busy. I don't think it matters much what they do, as long as they are up and doing. I'm fortunate that I can do something that I enjoy so much and that energizes me.

Huntington Woods, Michigan

Marvin Nochman (b. 1921) and his wife, Lois, have been married fifty-two years. Marvin helped raise Lois' two daughters from a previous marriage. They have one son, Joseph, as well as two grandchildren and four great-grandchildren.

Harry Steinberg
Age 95
Sculptor

I was a medical doctor by training and profession although all my life I was interested in creating things. I was a major in the Army Medical Corps for five years early in my medical career. During World War II, I worked in mobile hospital units moving forward with the troops throughout the European theatre. I was one of the doctors who treated the wounded in a makeshift hospital on a hill overlooking Omaha Beach the day after the Normandy invasion.

After I left the Service, my first wife and I and our three children moved from the East Coast to Los Angeles. I specialized in Ear, Nose and Throat Medicine and opened a private practice in Santa Monica. We bought a house in Westwood with a small pool in the back. One day, back in the 1960s, it occurred to me that it would be a wonderful thing to have some sort of a sculpture at the end of the pool. I pictured a woman with a water pot in her hand with water flowing out of it. My vision of the sculpture indicated how spare my knowledge of art was at the time.

A friend, who was working in the art field, took me to see the work of two sculptors, Michael and his wife Claire Hanzakos. I was fascinated when I saw their work. I purchased one of their pieces and I knew then and there that this was something I would love to do. That was the start of it for me. I studied with both of them and we became good friends.

Michael became very ill with cancer and needed to travel from his home to Santa Monica for treatment. I suggested that he and Claire come and stay with us, which they did. About the same time, my wife, Pat, had developed symptoms of what we now know was Alzheimer's. In those days no one knew what was happening to her. Claire took care of both of them during the day while I was at work. Both Michael and Pat died and Claire and I married in 1979.

My son, Peter, who is a builder and architect, constructed a studio for us behind our house where Claire could teach sculpture classes and where both of us could work. The studio became a center for a community of artists. The community includes past and present students from Claire's sculpture classes as well as sculptors who use the studio. It is an organic group and many have been coming here for at least twenty years. It is a lively, stimulating place and we all learn from each other. Many of the people who work here find it a very calming and healing experience. Claire and I work together to run the studio; it is a partnership.

I retired from my medical practice in 1984 when I was seventy-four years old, although I did some part-time teaching at UCLA until 1986. For many years I was a weekend artist. During that period, I sometimes incorporated my medical knowledge into my sculpture; for instance I would integrate body parts into some of the pieces. I moved fully into sculpture once I retired. I was fortunate that it was an already established part of my life.

My work is both traditional and very non-traditional. I work in clay and an offshoot of that has been sculpture made from found objects. People now bring me all sorts of objects such as wood, glass and metal to use. Sometimes I think they are cleaning out their attics for me. It has become a challenge and an adventure to take objects and change them into something else. The results are often fanciful. This endeavor has resulted in my work being carried by the Gallery of Functional Art, as well as other galleries in Los Angeles. In addition, my daughter got both Claire and me interested in jewelry making, and I think the type of jewelry we make is unique.

I keep trying new things and I'm not standing still. I still feel emotional excitement about my work and I look forward to each day and the joy of creation. I think my longevity and good health is due to the good genes I inherited from my parents but also from the physical energy I derive from the way I live. I'm also fortunate to be in touch with people whose work is different than mine and who are exciting and stimulating. My doctor recently asked about my physical exercise regimen and if I am walking enough. I told him I get my exercise carrying fifty-pound bags of clay in the studio as well as carrying sculpture one hundred fifty or two hundred feet to the kiln.

Our house and garden is filled with our work as well as the sculpture, masks and pots we have collected. Museum and university groups frequently come to tour our house and grounds to see the art. Our children have stayed with us at the house at various times and we often have parties here. Claire is presently sending out invitations for a party to celebrate my ninety-fifth birthday.

Claire and two other artists, Kaija Keel and Jilda Schwartz, have an exhibit showing in Los Angeles entitled *Face to Face*. They have done one hundred life-sized busts in clay of World War II veterans as they look today. Under their clay likenesses are their photos from the war. The veterans all sat for their portraits at our studio. Claire's colleague, Jilda Schwartz, did my portrait and it was one of the first ones completed. Everyone thinks it is a good likeness. Initially it was a shock to me as I envision myself as looking younger. The exhibit is intended as a tribute to all World War II veterans and it is a knockout—people cry when they see it.

Los Angeles, California

Harry Steinberg was born in 1910 in Pittsburgh and was one of five children of immigrant parents. He worked his way through college and medical school. He had a twin brother, who was also a physician, and a lover and collector of art. Two of Harry's children survive and he has three grandchildren. Claire Hanzakos (b. 1930) has one son.

4

Community Service
"Giving Back"

In his theory of the eight stages of man, the influential psychologist, Erik Erikson, introduced the term "generativity," to describe one of the important tasks of later life.[1] Generativity was initially defined as unselfishly guiding the next generation. It has now been interpreted more broadly as caring for or "giving back" to others.

A number of individuals in previous chapters "gave back" by participating in community and public service activities. In chapter two, the activities of Doris Sperling, Henry Foster, Carleen McGinn and Shirley Caldwell Patterson were extensions of lifelong service-oriented careers. In chapter three, some of the artists and craftsmen, such as Carrie Lo, Tyrone Smith and David Herzig, were committed to giving back via adjunct activities such as teaching, coaching, and philanthropy. Seven of the nine people presented in this chapter are involved in volunteer public or community service, which started or expanded in retirement and is now an integral part of their lives.

In addition to volunteerism in retirement, two people in this chapter are giving back via employment in second careers. Donald Majors, age sixty, is the youngest person presented in this book. His story exemplifies the emergent trend among fifty and sixty year olds to start new and different careers after early retirement. These second careers, which are often service oriented, may extend into later life. A second person in this category, Barbara Jean Jones, works at a state-supported human services agency helping relatives who are caregivers. She is a grandmother raising a granddaughter and she uses her experience to help others in similar situations. Her story is included, not only because of her employment, but because I think older grandparents who are the primary caregivers of their grandchildren perform a growing and important, but often overlooked and insufficiently supported, service in our society.

Marc Freedman, the founder and director of Civic Ventures, a non-profit organization that promotes meaningful second careers for older people, and author of *Prime Time*[2] and *Encore*,[3] compellingly presents the position that present-day older Americans are a natural resource (an asset rather than a burden) that society should tap for civic involvement. They have: the time (something that everyone else in America seems to lack), the wisdom and practical knowledge gained from a lifetime of experience, and the desire to give back and leave a legacy. Freedman sees matching the resources of older Americans with the human resource needs of American communities as being a win-win proposition. He perceives a deep hunger on the part of older Americans to live lives that matter and make use of their experience and knowledge.

Many of the people in this book are fulfilling Freedman's vision—they are creating new roles for themselves and making meaningful, sometimes innovative, service contributions in their communities, and beyond.

1. Molly Agras
   Fundraiser for a Homeless Shelter
   Interior Designer

2. Donald Majors
   Director of Special Projects, Constituent Services
   Office of U.S. Congressman Jim Cooper

3. Lois Schwartz
   Music Chair of the University of Michigan Entertainment
   Coalition "Auntie Mame"

4. Barbara Jean Jones
   Second Generation Parent
   Staff Consultant to Relative Caregiver Program and
   Co-facilitator of Relative Caregivers Support Group

5. William Valenzuela
   Community Leader
   Tuscon Chamber of Commerce Man of the Year
   Hispanic Chamber of Commerce Man of the Year

6. Joy Scott
   United Nations Association Volunteer

7. Berdelle Taylor Campbell
   Multi-faceted Community Advocate

8. Helen Hill
   Activist for the Mentally Ill
   Author and Memoir Writing Teacher

9. Fred Hoshiyama
   Community Leader
   Fundraiser

Molly Agras
Age 72
Fundraiser for a Homeless Shelter
Interior Designer

I sold my business at age sixty and started a new life. It turned out to be the most fortunate thing I ever did. But for the first six months I thought, "My god, what am I going to do, what is there left for me?" I had no specific retirement plan in mind. For fifteen years I had owned and operated a store, the Courtyard Collection, in downtown Palo Alto. I led a vigorous life and had to go abroad at least four times a year to buy large containers of artifacts from Thailand, Indonesia, Hong Kong and England in order to stock the store. I had reached a point, prior to selling the shop, where I felt I was doing too much, particularly since I had developed rheumatism. My children were getting married, having babies; I had a busy husband—and I simply wasn't making enough time for them.

I had gone through an earlier transition when I was age forty-five. At that time I had two children in college, two teenagers at home, and I decided it was time to start looking for what I was going to do. I had a British nursing degree and I would have had to go back to school to retrain. I never really liked nursing and went into it to please my parents. I decided to get a job as a salesperson at an antique store because I loved antiques. I loved the furniture, loved pleasing people and found I could sell things right off the wall. One extremely wealthy customer was interested in stockpiling imported antiques and he offered me a job. One day he rang up from France and asked if my passport was in order, as he wanted me to go to Morocco to buy rugs for his chateau. Doesn't it sound like a fairy tale? I went with twenty thousand dollars strapped to my body to buy the rugs.

While I was there, by some fluke, I met this man who was a rug expert and historian. He invited me to move into his house, which felt okay, since he was gay. One day he said, "Let's take off to the mountains for five days and buy some rugs and I'll show you some real folk art." We went up to the mountains in this rickety car and had a blast. My importing days started there and then and eventually led to the opening of my store. I am a risk taker and I'm lucky that my husband has always been able to support us, which has made it possible for me to take risks.

After I sold my store, I started to take up yoga for my rheumatism and found it fabulous. I now do yoga every day for at least one half hour and every spring I go on a yoga retreat in Mexico. Yoga has kept my rheumatism in check and I've been able to take myself off prescription medication. In addition to yoga, I swim forty laps early in the morning four times a week. I wear a wetsuit in the winter as I swim in an outdoor pool all year round. Yoga and swimming have made a big difference in my physical aging.

About the time I started feeling really great, all of my old customers started calling, saying, "You've left us in the lurch." My shop had been set up as a lovely house and that led to a particular interior design look that my customers liked. So I started doing freelance work, accepting commissions to do both large and small interior design projects. I did houses in Philadelphia, apartments in New York, as well as many houses here, a lot of them for the Packard family who like my artifacts. My larger projects involved furnishing whole houses. When I turned seventy, I decided I was again getting too busy and needed to cut back. I'm now doing smaller, local, interior design projects. In the last three years I've turned more and more of my attention to fundraising for the Opportunity Center in Palo Alto.

The building for the Opportunity Center is presently under construction. The Center will eventually provide housing and comprehensive social services under one roof for the homeless in the community. The services will be geared to people who have recently become homeless or are on the verge of becoming homeless. It is difficult for people to get back on their feet in this area, as housing is so expensive. The building will include ninety apartments for both individuals and families, and residents will be able to stay up to one or two years. One of the services offered during their stay will be employment assistance. The ground floor will also provide services such as food, toilets and showers for the chronically homeless. We hope the center will serve as a model for other communities. Fundraising has gone well and thus far we have raised twenty-five million dollars. In the process of fundraising, I've learned a lot about homelessness, the different types of homeless people and their different needs.

One of my fundraising events for the Center is held in my garden. We sell rugs from Oaxaca made by Mexican Indians. I've played a role in encouraging the Indians to make rugs with better colors and vegetable dyes for American consumers. The garden sale accomplishes two things: it helps the Zapotec weavers sell their rugs in the United States and a part of the profits from the sales go to the Center.

My husband and I are grateful for the good life we've had. We particularly appreciate it since we both suffered through the hardships of the Second World War in Europe. I was born and raised in Wales and met my husband, Stewart, who is a psychiatrist, when I was in nursing training in England. We immigrated to the United States and eventually came to Stanford University where Stewart has been on the medical faculty.

We have four children and are anticipating the birth of our sixth grandchild. We travel frequently, visiting our children, our families in England, as well as going on art and archeological tours, such as those sponsored by the Smithsonian.

I feel I have to give back and I try to do this by fundraising as well as generating interest and support in the community for the Opportunity Center.

Stanford, California

Author's Note: Another "creative ager" whom I interviewed led me to Molly. We met on a cold and rainy day for an early morning interview after she had returned from swimming laps at an outdoor pool. Molly had mentioned on the phone when we were trying to set up an interview time that she was leaving for Mexico in a few days to attend her annual, one-week yoga retreat. She was clearly looking forward to it and again mentioned it when we met.

A very dynamic woman, her extensive house is a testament to her eclectic and vibrant interior design taste. It is filled with rugs, furniture, and ethnic artifacts from Asia and Latin America, which she blends together beautifully, creating a warm, colorful and lively ambiance. The garden, where she holds her large and successful fundraisers, was filled with sculpture with a similar eclectic blend. I thought the Opportunity Center was very fortunate to have such an energetic and enthusiastic woman working on their behalf.

I found it interesting that Molly, similar to Shirley Caldwell Patterson in chapter two, had made a dramatic change as a result of a midlife quest. In both situations, it came at a time of decreasing maternal responsibilities and both women were able to tolerate risks taken along the way.

Donald Majors
Age 60
Director of Special Projects, Constituent Services
Office of U.S. Congressman Jim Cooper

I had no idea that coaching my son's Dixie Youth baseball team would eventually lead me to where I am today. I've made this transition, a strange one, from being a pipe fitter at Dupont to being a city councilman and now an assistant to a U.S. congressman.

My parents were very poor. There were five children in the family and we lived in a three-room shack with outdoor plumbing. My father worked at the Dupont Chemical plant in Nashville for thirty-eight years. Prior to 1962, African-Americans weren't allowed to work in what was called "operations," they could only work loading and doing cafeteria work. In 1962, Dupont started integrating the work force and my dad went from working in the kitchen to an operations job. The increase in salary was tenfold. Six months later my parents purchased a house with seven rooms and two bathrooms. We thought we had died and gone to heaven! I remember fighting with my brother to get into the bathtub. I was fifteen years old before I took my first bath in a real bathtub. We were the first African-Americans to live on the street and we were really intimidated as kids. All we did was sit on the porch and watch the people go by that first year. It took that long before we got accustomed to our surroundings.

I went to work at Dupont straight from high school. I worked in operations for four years and then took the test to get into the three-year pipe fitting apprentice program. The plant has miles and miles of pipes and pumps that require building, installing and maintenance. I was the first

African-American to be admitted into the apprenticeship program and the only African-American pipe fitter in the plant for seventeen years. It was not a lot of fun the first few years. My dad had been through all of this and was a good coach. For instance, I knew a lot more math than others in the apprenticeship program and he coached me to not look like I initially knew so much. It was the key to getting accepted. I worked at Dupont for thirty-seven years and retired when I came to work for Jim (Congressman Cooper).

My wife, Vallie, and I have been married for forty years and have two children. In 1977, we were living in an integrated neighborhood and a neighbor, who was a coach in the Dixie Youth Baseball Program, asked me to sign up my children as players, and myself as a coach. I was a little surprised since he was white, and the Dixie Youth program had been started specifically for white, rural youth. I got involved in the program and as the neighborhood changed and became predominantly African-American, so did the teams. I stayed with the athletic program for seventeen years and was program director for thirteen of those years. I liked what we were doing with the kids. Not only did we provide them with recreation, we instilled the importance of hard work, discipline, self-control and sportsmanship in our players. There were a number of kids being raised by single mothers and we were able to provide them with male role models.

We would have about forty kids at a time in the program. Over the years, I became known in the neighborhood and all the politicians in the city knew who I was because of the program. They would come down when they were running for office and would want me to help them out or endorse them. Finally, someone said to me, "Why are you always helping someone else out? Why don't you run for political office?" So in 1995, I decided to run for city council and I easily won.

I took a risk when I ran because of my lack of a college education and lack of political experience. Almost all city council members are college educated and at that time most were attorneys. As a result, I worked very hard and was driven to know more than most council members about every issue. I didn't want anyone to be able to say that I was not educated enough

to be on the council. I was something of a maverick and had a reputation for being analytic about every project that came up and I took a stand on every issue. I'm not a big fan of professional sports teams coming in and robbing the city and I spent nights going over pages of team contracts. I opposed the deals the city made with the football team and then the hockey team. I was outspoken but couldn't stop the deals. I'm particularly proud of the role I played in city council in getting a recycling program started in the city. I ran unopposed for my second term so I guess my constituency thought I was doing a good job.

I left the city council after eight years since it is mandated that after two terms, council members have to sit out one four-year term before running again. I enjoyed those eight years, as the council work was so different from my work at Dupont. I had continued working as a pipe fitter since the council job was part time and the pay was minimal.

I had apparently established a reputation as a city council member and one of Jim Cooper's friends suggested that I meet him. I did, and as a result I decided to help him with his election bid. He then chose to hire me as part of his staff when he was elected in 2003. Nine hundred people applied for eleven positions in this office. I was the only one without a college education and I told Jim I didn't have one. That was okay with him and he said he thought I had more to offer than most college graduates.

My official title is Special Director, which is actually a catchall. My main work is with constituent services. We have a large constituency in Nashville and a lot of people have problems with various federal agencies. I'm the person who connects with those agencies and helps solve constituents' problems. Some people call with local government issues rather than federal issues but I can still help them because of my prior experience in city government. That's a big plus for our office. My objective is to help people when they call as well as make them feel good about making the call. I also go out and make presentations on behalf of the congressman when he is away in Washington. Basically, that is enough to keep me very, very busy. I love the work and I have great respect for the congressman.

I would like to stay in this position for several more years. I think Jim will keep getting reelected for as long as he wants. Once I retire, I'll probably run again for city council. I'd like to have the opportunity to address the problems in the public school system, which include low performing inner-city schools and a lot of white flight.

I have the gift of being a good communicator, which helped in my work as a councilman and now in my present position. I think I got the gift from my dad. In looking back, I see that the leadership role I took in the youth athletic program led to the city council, which in turn led to my present job. I guess I took the steps, along with the risks, when the opportunities came my way. I also believe I have been blessed. It is not usual for a person from my background to be in my present position. I'm also blessed with good health. I like each and every day. I look ahead to the next day as something different always happens. I look forward to working during the week, to golf on Saturday and church on Sunday. I couldn't be happier at this point in my life. I wouldn't change a thing. It has been a blessed trip through life.

Nashville, Tennessee

Don Majors, born in 1946, is in the oldest group of baby boomers. He and his wife have a son and daughter and two granddaughters. They all live in Nashville.

Lois Schwartz
Age 70
Music Chair of the
University of Michigan Entertainment Coalition
"Auntie Mame"

What I am presently doing for the music school (University of Michigan School of Music) is evolving, and that is part of the pleasure of it all. How it came about is such a wild story. Three years ago, I received a formal invitation from the President of the University and Dean of the School of Music, inviting me to a dinner party at the Metropolitan Opera with William Bolcom and Arthur Miller, to celebrate the debut of their opera, *A View from the Bridge*. Bill Bolcom is on the music school faculty and Arthur Miller was an alumnus of the University. I thought that though I would love to go, it would probably cost me a fortune. I then received a phone call from the director of development at the music school who said she was doing a head count and asked if I was planning to attend. I said it depended on what it was going to cost me and she was taken aback, and said, "Oh, no, you are a guest of the President and Dean." I said, but I don't know them and besides I'm not rich. She insisted they would love to have me.

I later found out that they had done a computer search of University of Michigan alumni in the New York City area who regularly buy opera tickets, and my name kept coming up on their lists. They probably did assume I was well heeled; I later joked that I guess they hadn't found out that my seats were always in the balcony. Their search also revealed that I had been a president of a company (they didn't know it was a company of one operating out of my home), that I was on the Boards of American Opera

147

Projects and The Victor Herbert Foundation, and that I had written a book. I did go to the dinner and it turned out that I knew, or had some connection to, quite a few of the guests. So the people from the school learned quickly that I was very gregarious, that I was reasonably well connected, and was skilled at networking.

The dinner was in December and the following April I was in Ann Arbor and met with the music school's development officer. I told her I wanted to do something for the school but didn't know what, and then all of a sudden it hit me. I've fashioned myself after Auntie Mame and my sister's kids and their friends still think of me as their eccentric Auntie Mame.

I said I know what I can do. Just tell the faculty who have students who are about to graduate and move to New York City that there is this mildly eccentric woman who is well connected in the music world. She can serve as a welcoming committee, take them to dinner, drag them to new musical events, and help them get connected with people in the music world. George Shirley, who was a tenor at the Metropolitan Opera and is presently the director of the school's vocal program, thought it was a wonderful idea. I've now had over 120 kids who have made contact and it is still growing. I try to make them feel at home and connect them to people who can be useful to them. I'm their cheerleader and support person and they frequently want me to meet their parents when they come into town. I realize that I'm old enough to be a parent to their parents!

About a year after I started doing all of this, the New York chapter of the University of Michigan Entertainment Coalition (UMEC) was looking for a music chair. I took over the job as it fit so well with what I was already doing. Part of that job involves organizing panel discussions and breakfasts to help recent graduates find their way in the music world and help them advance their careers. We have a web site that gives information about alumni performances in and around New York, how to get tickets, etc.

There are a number of ideas that we would like to develop. One involves creating a buddy or mentor system, teaming up established alumni in the music world with recent graduates new to the city. I'd also like to establish an emergency fund for such things as plane tickets for out-of-town auditions. We're thinking of sponsoring an evening event called *Meet the Michigan Musicians* and inviting area alumni interested in music to hear some of these performers. Those invited might also be potential donors to the school.

I've had many different jobs in my life that may not seem related but one thing I've enjoyed in all of them is putting people together. I'm like a matchmaker. I just love it when I put extraordinary people together and they hit it off. I love what I'm presently doing and it goes hand in hand with my long-term love of music. I'm having a wonderful time.

I was exposed to opera, particularly Wagner, as a sophomore in high school and I've loved opera ever since. In fact, one reason I went to Michigan was because there was a course on Wagner. My parents loved music and exposed my sister, Anne, and me to a lot of music at home. I've played the piano, violin and trumpet. I consider myself a spiritual person and music is often a spiritual and transcendental experience for me.

My employment history includes working in publishing, freelance writing, radio and TV production and educational programming. My career evolved from those jobs into designing and developing training programs. I found the instructional technology field was made for me; I could use both sides of my brain and each training program I designed was different. I started my own corporation, Esprit Consulting Corporation, in 1972 and ran it for twenty-six years. I dissolved it in 1998 when I was sixty-three years old. I was able to retire because of a pension fund and the fact that I live in a rent-controlled apartment in the city.

I started getting a little bored with work when I was in my fifties and around that time I attended a panel discussion (Beverly Sills, was one of the panelists) on the need for business professionals in the arts. Things clicked for me at that point and I saw a new path for myself. I volunteered at the New York City Opera and was getting ready to attend N.Y.U.'s Art Administration Program when I was diagnosed with breast cancer. I had a mastectomy in 1990 at age fifty-five. It made me hesitant about spending so much money at N.Y.U. so I attended the Arts Administration Program at Marymount College instead. My internship for the program was at American Opera Projects, an organization that encourages young composers and commissions and develops new works of opera. I eventually became a board member and did a considerable amount of volunteer work for them. Though I continue to be supportive of the organization, I resigned from the board and volunteer responsibilities when I had my second diagnosis of breast cancer. The second mastectomy in 2001 was eleven years after the first and I was sixty-six at the time.

I was searching to do something that had meaning to me after my recuperation and the invitation to that dinner was the start of something new. Breast cancer, along with the death of friends who were my contemporaries, not only makes me aware of my mortality, but also makes me live more in the present and do the things that are meaningful to me. I celebrate my age and the fact that I have survived.

In addition to keeping contact with a huge circle of friends, I devote a good deal of time to physical fitness. I walk a lot, attend a stretch class, work with a personal trainer once a week and swim three times a week. For me, swimming is like meditating.

I never married and decided that I was not going to be a "spinster" but was going to enjoy life. My only regret is that I never had children of my own. Someone recently told me that I have touched so many young lives-- my niece and nephews, the children of friends and all the young musicians I have nurtured. I hope that is the case.

New York City

Lois Schwartz (b. 1935) grew up in New York City and has resided there most of her life. She is a graduate of the University of Michigan and attended the London School of Economics. She was a recipient of the University of Michigan's Distinguished Alumni Service Award, which she received in a ceremony in Ann Arbor in 2007.

Barbara Jean Jones
Age 67
Second Generation Parent
Staff Consultant to Relative Caregiver Program and
Co-facilitator of Relative Caregivers Support Group

My daughter Katrina, Ebony's mother, made some bad choices relatively early in her life. She started using drugs when she was about sixteen or seventeen years old, which led to her eventually becoming addicted to crack cocaine. It is truly a horrible addiction that is very hard to overcome. I had worked for years as a counselor at Meharry's drug and alcohol program here in Nashville but when the problem came to my own doorstep, I wasn't able to help my child. Katrina managed to get through high school with a lot of pushing and shoving but her drug use progressed and her disappearances from home occurred with greater frequency. I'd go out looking for her and bring her home when I could find her. She would rest, eat well and then go back out on the streets. In the course of that happening, she came home one day and said to us, "I think I'm pregnant." Going through my mind was, "Oh no, oh no, oh no, what can I do. I haven't done a good job with Katrina and here comes a baby who is probably going to have an addiction, and might have physical impairments, and God only knows what else." But we (my second husband, Joe, and I) said we are going to do this and we took care of Katrina during her pregnancy.

Katrina went into labor earlier than anticipated and our granddaughter, Ebony, was a preemie and weighed just four pounds at birth. My primary concern was the possible effects of drugs on her but our doctor assured us she was fine. I was fifty years old when all this happened. I just assumed

I would keep and raise Ebony. I didn't go through any big decision-making process about it. There was really never a time in my mind when I thought she would go anywhere but to my home. My parents and all my brothers and sisters had passed away by then and I was the only one left. I thought, "She is part of my family, she is my grandbaby and who could better raise her?" People were astonished by my decision and said things like, "You're going to raise a baby at your age? This is your time in life, you've had your children." I have never regretted my decision. Ebony has been nothing but a blessing to me, an absolute blessing. There have been ups and downs but I can truthfully say life has been a joy with her.

Raising Ebony has given me a second chance. Because of her circumstances, I've raised her with extra care, with extra protection, and I've made extra effort to leave no stone unturned. We talk about everything. I think she feels safe and she knows she is loved. She and I have a very strong bond. She calls me "granny" as do all her friends. My husband, Joe, adored her and loved her as if she were his biological grandchild. Ebony was so attached to him. He passed away when she was seven and she and I made it through together, we endured. Joe and I had been married for twelve years when he died.

Ebony is now sixteen years old and is talented and intellectually gifted. She attends the Nashville School for the Arts, a magnet school, which she auditioned for in both music and theater. The city doesn't provide transportation to magnet schools so I drive Ebony back and forth to school across town. I tackle the interstate twice a day, every single school day. I've always organized my work schedule around Ebony's schedule.

A number of years ago, there was a young man in my church who sought me out every Sunday and would say to me, "We need you in our program, we need your wisdom, Ms. Barbara." I didn't really listen to what the program was about. He kept after me and finally, to get him off my back, I agreed to listen. He told me about the Relative Caregiver Program, a new program the state was sponsoring. It sounded interesting so I consented to go for an interview. The woman who interviewed me immediately offered me a consulting position. I've served in that capacity for the last four years.

Part of the job involves giving advice to the social work staff from the perspective of a relative who is caring for a child. Relatives, particularly grandparents, don't necessarily need or want to be taught how to rear their grandchildren. They've done that; they've had the experience. What they want is to be heard, to have their needs understood. The emotional, physical and financial stresses and strains on these families are enormous. One woman in the program had to take in nine grandchildren!

In addition to consulting with staff, I've been a co-facilitator of an ongoing support group. So many of the people in the group have children who are addicted, or are in prison or are deceased. The group is a place where they can safely express their feelings—I'm hurting, angry, lonely, isolated, overwhelmed and exhausted. There is a healing process when people with similar problems come together and share their feelings. People have told me how much I've helped them. I've tried to give them a sense of hope.

For years, Katrina would come and go and was unable to bond with Ebony. She is now in her second year of treatment at Magdalene House, a residential rehabilitation program in Nashville for women with a history of drug abuse and prostitution. It is a wonderful program. We now get to see her often and she usually comes to church with us on Sundays. One of the things I've learned is that people remain stuck in their functioning at the chronological age at which they began abusing drugs. So Katrina and Ebony are pretty much at the same developmental level at this point. They now spend time together and are developing a relationship. It is wonderful to see that happening and I feel very good that I've helped to nurture it.

I try to take good care of myself. I suffer from fibromyalgia. I don't let it tell me what I can and can't do. I won't allow physical things that attack my body to bring me down. Religion also helps me cope. Going back to my childhood, religion has been a guiding force in my life. I have always had a sense of a higher power and that sense has grown as I've grown. I belong to a wonderful, supportive congregation with an inspirational minister, the Mount Zion Baptist Church. I have passed on my profound sense of religion and spirituality to Ms. Ebony.

I was born in Nashville in 1939 and I've lived here all of my life. My family was poor; I'm still poor. I was one of six children and alcoholism and tuberculosis ran in the family. My father was an alcoholic and I had a brother and sister who died of alcoholism. As a result, I made a decision early in my life to avoid alcohol. I married my first husband, Lewis, when I was sixteen and the marriage eventually ended in divorce. In addition to Katrina, my two sons, John and Lewis, are from that marriage. Both of them live in Nashville and are very supportive of Ebony. I now have eight grandchildren (twins run in the family and both sons have twins) and nine great-grandchildren.

I quit school when I married and later went back and got my high school diploma. Many years after that, I attended Tennessee State University. In fact, I went to T.S.U. at the same time as my youngest son. I completed two years of course work and specialized in social welfare. I've always worked and most of my work experience has been in the social welfare field. Ebony has been the center of my life for sixteen years and I know it will be difficult for me when she leaves home for college. I've been thinking that I might go back to school then and finally get my college degree.

People ask me what it feels like to be sixty-seven; all I can say is that I'm grateful I'm still here. I'm looking forward to eighty-three. I don't know why I've picked that age but I know that I want to still be going and doing and useful at that age. I think my sense of purpose propels and motivates me to keep going. I strongly believe that the key to longevity is feeling useful and needed.

Nashville, Tennessee

William G. Valenzuela
Age 74
Community Leader
Tucson Chamber of Commerce Man of the Year
Hispanic Chamber of Commerce Man of the Year

There was a group of us kids, Hispanic kids, here in Tucson, who joined the Marine Corps Reserves in 1948 and 1949. Our fathers, uncles, and cousins had all served in the military during World War Two. The Korean War started in 1950 and we were activated and sent to Camp Pendleton. I had just turned seventeen when I started boot camp. I volunteered three times to be sent to Korea to join my buddies from Tucson but they never sent me. I'm thankful now because our guys were shot up pretty bad and we lost twelve of our Tucson buddies.

I was nineteen when I got out of the service. I thought I was a big shot and I didn't want to go back and finish the last two years of high school. I had trained as a machinist in the service and when I got out I wanted to learn a trade and eventually have my own business. I realized it was going to be hard because I didn't have the education.

I applied for a drywall job on a building project. The superintendent, who was looking for someone with experience in drywall, immediately realized I had none. He asked, "Are you Hispanic?" When I answered yes, he replied, "We don't want Hispanics to learn the trade, they'll ruin the wages." I said, "Just give me a break. I just got out of the service, I recently got married, and I can learn what you want me to know in a week." He gave me a break and they made it so hard for me that I had a fever for the first six months. But I was determined to learn the trade and I stuck with it. In the end, it turned out to be a really good thing for me.

157

After that I went to work for a drywall company. I worked real hard for them and eventually became a vice president and partner in the company. My children were growing up and I wanted my own business. I wanted to pass something on to them and make their lives easier than mine. I started this company, W.G. Valenzuela Dry Wall, in 1979. I put all my effort into the business and it snowballed and snowballed. I was able to bring in my family to work here—my son, my five daughters and their husbands, and it has become a family affair. Even my granddaughters work here part-time, after school and in the summers. We expanded in 1997 and added a paint store, Sunbelt Coatings. At one time the business had up to three hundred sixty employees.

Back in those earlier days, banks wouldn't lend to Hispanics and thought we were bad risks. They also wouldn't lend to contractors. Lo and behold, when my business was doing real well, local bankers approached me about lending me money. My accountant encouraged me to borrow from the bank saying, "You have to get a credit line. You're a big boy now, and you have to do it like a businessman." Soon after I borrowed money and was using it, higher up officials in the bank than the ones I had dealt with stopped the loan even though I wasn't behind one minute in my payments. It put me in a tight, difficult situation and I quickly had to work out a plan to pay back the loan, which I did. I later found out they had stopped all loans to contractors. It taught me a fabulous lesson—to pay as I go and never use the bank's money.

Other people found themselves in similar situations with the banks, and the way I had handled the fiasco became known in the community. As a result, I was invited to join the Greater Tucson Economic Council. I'll never forget the first time I went to a meeting. I saw all these professors and big bankers and the mayor, and my hands started sweating, my armpits were soaking wet and I thought, "What the hell am I doing here? What do I know about any of this?" My son had dropped me off and I had no car with me or I would have left. There were thirty people there and we each were asked to contribute three ideas about how to help the economy in Tucson. They kept debating all the ideas and eliminating the bad ones.

At the end, the two remaining ideas that hadn't been rejected turned out to be mine. I thought this isn't so bad after all. That was the start of my involvement in community service.

I always used to hire National Guard and Reserve people; I usually had seven or eight of them at a time working for me. The next thing I know, I was invited to join the Arizona Committee of the Employer Support of the Guard and Reserve (ESGR), which functions under the Department of Defense. It is an organization that promotes cooperation and understanding between the National Guard and Reserve members and their civilian employers, and assists in resolving conflicts arising from the employee's military commitments. I've now been in this work for over twenty years and I have served as chairman of the committee. In fact, seventy percent of my time was devoted to ESGR when I was chairman of the state committee. The Department of Defense has given me two awards and one of them is the Roche Award for my work with ESGR.

My volunteer efforts for the military expanded. I worked with the Secretary of the Army helping to recruit high school dropouts, mainly Hispanics, into an educational and training program from which they could then qualify to join the service. I've been in the Army Reserve Ambassadorship Program, which primarily lobbies Congress for the needs of the Army Reserve. Over the years, I've spearheaded fundraising to send fourteen- to seventeen-year-old boys and girls to Marine Corps summer camp. The sense of discipline and responsibility the kids acquire is wonderful. And I've served on the Civilian Support Committee to defend the National Guard 162nd Fighter Wing Base from closure.

My other community activities to improve the quality of life here in Tucson include: Chairmanship of the Tucson Airport Authority, Chairmanship of the Tucson Metropolitan Chamber of Commerce, membership on the Boards of Directors of Habitat for Humanity, University of Arizona Heart Association, Southern Arizona Homebuilders Association, Southern Arizona Minutemen and the Compass Bank. For sixteen years I was active in the Pascua Yaqui Indian Apprenticeship Program. We helped train young men and women, many who had not completed high school, in the building trades. The program is presently in less demand as many of the Indians now work in the Casino.

I had a heart attack six years ago. Since then, although I'm still in charge of some projects, my kids have taken over the day-to-day operation of the business. Two-and-a-half years ago I decided to get away from all the community responsibilities, spend more time with my wife and do more traveling. I got off lots of Boards and then I started to feel depressed. I would find myself sitting at my desk with nothing to do but read the mail. I went back to working for ESGR and other organizations and since then I've felt a lot better. I'd say that now I spend more than fifty-five percent of my time in community service.

I'm asked to give a lot of speeches. At first public speaking was very difficult for me but with time I've become more comfortable with it. When I talk to Hispanic audiences I speak from the heart and try to offer inspiration and encouragement. I came from a poor background, I didn't have a good education, but I had a strong work ethic and worked real hard to get where I am. I've always wished that I had a better formal education. When I was seventy years old, the Board of Education granted me a high school diploma in honor of the community work I have done. It made me cry.

My religion (Roman Catholic) and my family are extremely important to me. My wife, Celina, and I have been married for fifty-five years. We started going steady when she was thirteen and I was fourteen. We are a close-knit family and do everything together. In addition to raising five daughters and one son, we have seventeen grandchildren and nine great- grandchildren.

Many of my friends who have slowed down say to me, "Are you crazy? Why are you doing all of this? You should be taking it easy and be out on the golf course." What I do consumes a lot of time and sometimes involves big decisions. But it is where I think I belong. All the awards I get like *Man of the Year* and others that hang in the office don't mean that much to me. What is important is that the organizations I work with, and the things I do, end up helping people.

Tucson, Arizona

Joy Scott
Age 73
United Nations Association Volunteer

I guess you might call me a "late bloomer." About three-and-a-half or four years ago, when I was sixty-eight or sixty-nine years old, I saw a plea embedded in an article in a local newspaper for volunteers for the United Nations Association gift shop in Palo Alto. I responded to the request, although initially I didn't intend to become as involved as I am now. I didn't have a specific plan for this stage in my life. I knew I wanted something of my own and I didn't just want to make money nor did I just want to design jewelry, though that is something I love to do. I wanted to be involved in something with a deeper, far-reaching goal. The United Nations Association and the UNA gift shop fit that and came at just the right time.

The UNA gift shop is sponsored by the local UNA chapter, which has about 350 members. The Association plays a fundraising role as well as an educational role in the community, providing information about the UN and world issues and events. We support a lending library in the shop, which is available to the public, and people who come into the shop often engage in discussions about current events and the UN. The gift store sells UNICEF products from the UNICEF catalogue as well as artifacts from developing countries. We try to buy fair trade products, which means the artisans are fairly paid, as well as paid on time. There used to be several hundred UN gift shops across the country, often called UNICEF shops. Now there are only seven. Our store provides the largest amount of financial support to UNICEF of all the stores, aside from the one located at the UN building.

The shop is run entirely by volunteers. There are fewer and fewer of us

these days and we are getting older. My responsibilities at the shop have grown over the years. I'm one of a team of four managers and buyers. I know a great deal about fabrics, textiles of all kinds, and most recently the woven rugs, the kilims. I'm also interested in ethnic jewelry and I've been designing and making jewelry for many years. Jewelry buying is one of the things I'm in charge of at the store. Our team of buyers often goes on buying trips together, which is great fun. A lot of our contacts are former Peace Corps members who are still interested in helping developing communities. My other responsibilities include training new volunteers, doing the bookkeeping for the store, decorating the store's interior as well as planting and taking care of the outside window boxes. I work one or two shifts a week as a salesperson and I'm on the Board of Directors of the local UNA chapter. My position allows me to play a liaison role between the Board and the volunteers at the store. I put in a considerable amount of time each week and it is where my heart is, in supporting the UNA and the United Nations.

A gate opened for me when I responded to the newspaper article. In looking back, I can see that my long-term ideological commitments and life and work experiences laid the groundwork for what I am doing now. I've always had concern for the needy, for the disadvantaged, for people who can't care for themselves. My husband and I were keen supporters of Eleanor Roosevelt and the work and ideals of the UN. My concern for the children of the world is powerful. As a mother, and now as a grandmother, my concern is even keener. My other strong interest is in the environment. We need to live lightly on Mother Earth. The UN addresses these concerns, caring for, and supporting life. I've been involved in other volunteer work but I can't think of any other volunteer activity that would pull on my heartstrings like this one.

For many years, when my three children were small, I organized and oversaw the UNICEF Trick or Treat project on the Stanford University campus. It was a big project and we had lots of community support and help. I would speak at elementary school assemblies and tell the children about the UNICEF projects their donations and fundraising efforts helped to support. It was very gratifying. My children are now in their forties, and two years ago, a young mother pushing a stroller saw me and remembered me from those days saying, "You are the UNICEF lady." Once my children grew older and I returned to graduate school and employment, UNICEF activities stopped being a major focus. I did, however, do considerable individual gifting to UNICEF, kept myself informed about UNICEF projects and joined the local UNA chapter in 1995.

I grew up in Kansas. My father was the Director of Nature Studies for the city of Manhattan, Kansas, and also a science teacher. He was a Quaker who was involved in peace activities, was concerned about environmental issues as well as the inequities of the world. So the seeds of my ideological commitments were planted early.

I attended a small Presbyterian college in Kansas. There was no art department there and I think I would have majored in art if there had been. The closest I could come was Home Economics, which offered costume design courses. So I prepared to teach Home Economics after I graduated from college in 1954. I did do that for one year.

I had already met my future husband and we married the following year. We moved to Chicago where he had a fellowship at the University of Chicago. I had started taking courses in Library Science before the move and continued to do so in Chicago. I held jobs in school libraries in Chicago and later in California, after we moved here in 1960. I did not work outside the home once we started our family. I stayed home full time for sixteen years and it was a luxury to be able to do that.

I finally did go back to graduate school (the encouragement from my husband and children to do so had gotten louder) and received a degree in Library Science in 1982 from San Jose State University. After that I held positions as a librarian in academic and legal settings. Though my professional career has been as a librarian, for five years I did work in a shop that sold ethnic artifacts, rugs and jewelry, about which I became very knowledgeable. I also learned a lot about the decision-making process in running a business. That experience has helped me at the UNA store.

My health has been pretty darn good. I have no cartilage left in either knee so I have been working to strengthen the muscles and tendons around these joints. I walk daily, do stretching and strengthening exercises, and go to a weekly yoga class.

My husband, Richard, is my best friend and constant companion. We are in constant contact by phone or e-mail with our immediate family, and they are our strongest social group. We visit our three children and their families as often as possible—several times a year. Besides the family, I have a very close friend, Joanne, with whom I spend part of one day a week. Her friendship is important in my life. The other volunteers in the UNA shop are also important supportive connections for me. I have a wonderful neighbor just up the street—Connie. She is in her eighties, and she has taught me much about self-esteem, mindfulness, and enjoying ordinary small pleasures. I think she is sort of a mother figure for both my husband and me. We are her first contact when she has health or house troubles. We communicate often and share meals with her and Joanne regularly.

Richard and I start the day with a cup of coffee and an inspection stroll around our garden while still in pajamas and robe. This is a very important way to stay in touch with each other and with Mother Earth. There is never a day we are not in our garden.

I am not involved in any formal religious activities these days. I consider myself to be "spiritual" and very much in touch with "creative" and "life forces." The out-of-doors is where I feel closest to a "greater being," not in a ceremony or service. I am very serious about living lightly on Mother Earth and work actively to help save and protect the natural environment we are borrowing.

I'd say there are many advantages to being a late bloomer. It has been a wonderful life and we are still having a good time.

Stanford, California

Joy Scott (b. 1932) and her husband have celebrated their fiftieth anniversary. Richard, a social scientist, has been on the Stanford University faculty since 1960. The Scotts have three children and five grandchildren.

Berdelle Taylor Campbell
Age 79
Multi-faceted Community Advocate

Although I was involved in volunteer work before retirement, the opportunity of additional time after retiring allowed me to take on new civic responsibilities. While I was still working, I was aware of organizations and issues I supported and I would think, "I could help more if I wasn't working." I looked ahead to the things I could do in the community once I retired. I've become, essentially, a full-time volunteer, devoting my efforts to initiatives, causes, and problem-solving projects that I feel are very important.

I retired in 1995, at age sixty-eight, from the Tennessee Department of Health where I had worked for twenty-five years. My expertise was in Maternal and Child Health and my job responsibilities included planning, statistics, needs assessment, grant writing and program evaluation. Retirement day was especially festive as the mayor of Nashville declared the day I retired "Berdelle Taylor Campbell Day" and a Zelcova Elm tree was planted in the nearby park in my honor.

My husband, Ernest, and I have been residents of the Historic Germantown neighborhood in downtown Nashville for more than twenty-five years. When we moved here, people thought we were crazy, off our rocker. We had been living in Belle Meade (an affluent, exclusive, suburban neighborhood) and once our children left home we became interested in living in a different sort of place. We were particularly interested in inner-city historic neighborhoods because we were concerned about core city decay.

That was in 1979 and the Germantown neighborhood area had just

167

been listed on the National Register of Historic Places. The area, approximately 18-20 city blocks, established in the late 1840s and incorporated into the city of Nashville in 1865, contained a significant concentration of Victorian buildings. We drove over to look at the neighborhood and it was a heartbreaking trip; the area had become a total slum, the houses were tumbledown and it was prostitution row. We did however meet an interesting architect and historic preservationist who was living in Germantown. He had bought up property there and had plans to restore the neighborhood. We began to think about it and became excited and energized by the challenge and the concept of what could be done. We eventually bought a house, along with an adjoining vacant lot for a garden, and started the restoration process.

I didn't realize at the time, but I've been told since, that the fact that we (a Vanderbilt Professor and a Planner for the Department of Health) were here, gave the neighborhood credibility and was a statement of confidence in the future. The area was zoned for industrial use and we, along with some other homeowners, started buying vacant property with the goal of having the neighborhood rezoned for residential use. Eventually we were able to get a completely new zoning classification written and approved that made it possible to get the neighborhood rezoned for mixed use—residential and limited business.

We had lots of barriers and challenges to overcome. The biggest challenge occurred when a national company bought up an entire block (directly across the street from our restored house!) in order to build an auto emissions control station. We knew that a federal law protecting historic neighborhoods required an environmental impact study and that had not taken place. One weekend morning, the company's bulldozer started excavating, even though the company hadn't received a building permit. We couldn't reach anyone in city government and so a group of us started picketing and then we blocked the bulldozer. After the bulldozer operator notified his superior, the police arrived and said we had to let the work continue. But we persisted. We were arrested while the cameras captured my husband and me, two senior citizens, along with two neighbors, being taken to jail in a police car. It was on TV and in the newspapers for a week and brought the issue to the attention of the general public and the city administration. In the end, the company did not get a permit and Metro government bought the property. It never occurred to me that we wouldn't win. After that, other inner-city neighborhoods began contacting us for advice as they faced various similar problems. Our Germantown neighborhood has grown from a handful of families into the hundreds. We've become a model for other neighborhoods and all of this has contributed to the revitalization of the downtown. Ernest has served as President of the Germantown Neighborhood Association and I was Vice-President for many years.

While still employed, I was very active in Planned Parenthood and served in many different capacities, including local Board President, National Board member and delegate to the International Planned Parenthood Federation. I am still on the local advisory board. My other early community efforts included being a Commissioner on the Nashville Beautification Commission as well as serving on the Advisory Council to the Greenways Commission of Nashville.

At the time of my retirement, I was asked to join the Board of the League of Women Voters. I had avoided joining the League while I worked, as I knew how time-consuming League work could get. I became Environmental Committee Chair and have been in that role for eleven years. We monitor water and air quality and keep an ear out for legislation that relates to environmental issues. We work with the state legislators and, in the long run, I do believe we have a positive effect. We recently worked on a bottle deposit bill. The bill didn't pass and we are gearing up for the next session.

In 2003, I was able to organize and facilitate four public forums on sprawl, smart growth, land use and transportation. The interest the forums generated led to the formation of a regional planning body involving ten counties in middle Tennessee.

Voter Registration, another emphasis of the League of Women Voters, gets my priority participation because I know it is one of the League's most important functions. In 2004, I was the recipient of the annual Molly Todd Award (named after a founder of the Nashville League), in recognition of my voter registration and environmental work and my role in the establishment of the Tennessee Economic Council for Women.

After retirement, I devoted more time to a citizen's group called *Recycle! Nashville* and served as Vice-President for ten or eleven years. Our goals have been to promote sensible waste solutions through educational awareness and advocacy. Considerable success was realized and our volunteer efforts led the Metro government to add recycling to their trash pickup schedule.

I've been on the Board of Directors of the downtown YMCA for ten years. In addition to exercise and wellness facilities, the "Y" provides special projects for inner-city kids: summer camps, swimming lessons, after-school tutoring and help with homework. The Board raises the money to pay for these projects. I've been able to convince the Downtown "Y" to recycle and I'm now working on getting all 25 Middle Tennessee "Y"s to do the same.

The mayor has recently appointed me to a twenty-two-member task force to work on the redevelopment of Nashville's Cumberland River waterfront. Most all of the other members are representatives of official agencies or architects or planners. I think I am the only "citizen" member and I may actually have been the catalyst for the commission. A proposal to build a baseball stadium near the river was being pushed through prior to any public hearings about waterfront use. At a public meeting about the location of the stadium, I pointed out that although it was late in the game, there had been no public meetings for citizens to say what would be the best use for that section of the waterfront. I'm pleased to say that our task force convened three public meetings enabling hundreds of citizens to have input. The task force put together a design team and we hope for a draft of a Master Plan by the end of the year.

I'm fortunate that my health has been exceptional, requiring very little medication. I have experienced some hearing loss over the past decades and I will always be coping with that. Ernest and I walk and work out regularly at the "Y" fitness center and, in addition, we work in our garden. People often remark that they can't believe that Ernest and I are both in our 80th year. We stay so active in our neighborhood, our city and the bigger world.

Everything I do in the community relates to everything else I do; saving the inner city, historic restoration, green sustainable building, recycling, greenways, the significance of trees, the role of the river, what happens to the quality of our air and water, and citizen participation. The fact is that so much needs to be done to even maintain the quality of these things at the present level, not to mention improving them. I believe that if a person can contribute, he or she jolly well should. But I'm not doing it because I should. I'd be denying myself if I didn't participate as I get so much satisfaction out of what I do. I love this stage in my life. I've never had this much fun.

Nashville, Tennessee

Berdelle Taylor Campbell was born (1927) and raised in Mississippi. She received a Bachelor of Science from the University of South Mississippi and a Master of Science from the University of North Carolina School of Public Health. Berdelle and her husband, Ernest, have been married fifty-seven years. They have four children and seven grandchildren. "My cup runneth over" was her response when asked how she feels about her present life.

Helen Hill
Age 90
Activist for the Mentally Ill
Author and Memoir Writing Teacher

When I retired from teaching at age sixty-eight in 1983, there were two things I wanted to do. One was to clean the attic and the other was to finish a book I had been working on sporadically for many years.

Those projects got put on hold when I became interested in improving the lives of people who suffer from a mental illness. It started in the fall after I retired, when my husband, Don, and I attended a seminar offered by two social workers at the Community Mental Health Center. The seminar was designed for people like us, who had a family member with a mental illness. We learned a good deal about mental illnesses and we also learned about a relatively new advocacy organization, the Alliance for the Mentally Ill, which has since become nationally known as NAMI. When the seminar ended in December, those of us attending didn't want to disband, as we had become a close-knit group. I suggested that we continue meeting at our house and in January, seven of us met around our dining table, and the local chapter of the Alliance was born. Don and I became very active in the organization. Don was the first president and I edited and produced the newsletter for eight years.

In 1985, I went to a NAMI conference where I learned about a clubhouse program in New York started by people who had previously been hospitalized with a mental illness. It had become a thriving organization—providing mutual support, helping people relearn lost skills and getting them back to work. In 1989, inspired by the clubhouse model, Don and I, with the help of others, started Trailblazers of Washtenaw. For twelve years, I was very active in the organization and was President of the Board for several years. My volunteer work became a full-time second career, dedicated to helping people with mental illness recover their lives as much as possible. I wrote grant proposals, was involved in fundraising, in educating the public, and in encouraging businesses to provide jobs. Other people have gradually taken over those responsibilities.

I did finally get the attic cleaned, although it did take quite a while. And I did finally finish my book, *A Proud and Fiery Spirit,* based on my grandfather's seafaring journals, which was published by the Duxbury Rural and Historical Society in 1995. My grandfather started keeping a journal in 1846 when he was fourteen and kept it up all his life. At the age of sixteen, he went to sea in a bark, a small vessel with three masts, and in the next thirteen years sailed all over the world. He made voyages to the Mediterranean, the Arctic, the Caribbean, around Cape Horn to San Francisco and home to Boston by way of the Pacific and Indian Oceans. While he was at sea he was very lonely and wrote his heart out. He read a lot and learned to write well.

My mother had inherited the journals, and after she died in the flu epidemic in 1918, they stayed in my father's attic. I became interested in them when I was sixteen, and though my father had earlier threatened to burn them because they were personal, they eventually came to me. I carried them with me wherever I lived, and finally began to transcribe them when my youngest child was four. In 1972, I received a grant from the National Archives that enabled me to do a lot of research for the book. Since its publication, I have transcribed the journals of the Civil War years, but I haven't done the years after the war when he left the sea and went back to the farm.

In 1992, Jim Robertson, a friend and neighbor who was teaching writing in the Learning in Retirement program at the University of Michigan's Turner Resource Center, told me they needed another teacher in the program and asked if I would be interested in teaching a weekly memoir-writing group. I've now been doing it for thirteen years. Leading this group has been a joy, for in writing about our lives we have come to know each other well and have become like an extended family. There are no specific assignments. People write what they choose and read their pieces aloud to the group. The only rules we have are no nitpicking about grammar and spelling and constructive criticism is welcome. After a couple of years, someone in the group said, "What's fair is fair. It's time for you to write something." I joined the group as a writer then and have enjoyed mining my own life since. I think the writing has meant a lot to all of us. You remember things you hadn't thought of for a long time and writing about them gives you perspective and understanding.

After attending a workshop on publishing books, I asked the group if they would like to do a book. I thought they would get pleasure out of seeing they had written things good enough to publish. At first the idea was daunting but working together on the book became an enjoyable experience. The other editors and I sometimes made editorial suggestions but we were interested in making changes only if the writing was unclear. We wanted the voices to be authentic. We worked at my dining room table where so many good things have happened. The book, *The Man Who Eats Snakes and Other Tales,* was published in 2001.

My husband of fifty-eight years died in 1997. My daughter and her family now live in San Diego and my three sons and their families live in and near Ann Arbor. I have five grandchildren and three great-grandchildren. We have frequent family gatherings for birthdays and holidays. These have always been held at my house and I'm pleased that my children have started holding some of these events at their homes. I'm interested in national and local politics and meet weekly with "the lunch bunch" to discuss politics.

I've always been physically active. Don and I had a farm outside of town where we labored at renovations and gardening but I sold that a couple of years after his death. I also did yoga for thirteen years but stopped before hip replacement surgery last year. I'm scheduled for a second hip replacement next month.

Five years ago, I wrote in a piece for the memoir group that I was banking on fifteen more years to complete my writing projects as well as other projects I had in mind. Life keeps getting in the way and I'm slower about getting things done than I used to be. I still need fifteen more years.

Ann Arbor, Michigan

———————

Helen Hill was born in Brooklyn, New York, in 1915. After the death of her mother when she was three, she moved with her father and two brothers to Taunton, Massachusetts, where her father's family had always lived. She was educated at Wheaton College, Brown University and the University of Illinois. For twenty years she taught writing and children's literature at Eastern Michigan University.

Fred Hoshiyama
Age 92
Community Leader
Fundraiser

I'm ninety-two years old, my hearing is failing and I'm legally blind. However, I feel good and I hope, God willing, I can reach one hundred. I still look forward to the future. My mother would use the term *oha'tsu,* which literally translated means the first fruit of the season. She would imply by using the term that something was a source of pleasure or a reason to celebrate life. I can still get that *oha'tsu* experience.

Through her sayings, my mother imparted her values to me. Among those sayings were *ga'man,* which translated from the Japanese means, hang in there, hope for a better tomorrow, and *gi'ri,* the best translation being pay back or give back to society. My mother taught me to remember that a person can't make it alone, somebody has helped either directly or indirectly. So when a person is able, he has an obligation to give back. Those two teachings have stayed with me since childhood; hang in there and enjoy life and use whatever God-given talent you have to give back. I've tried to live my life by these teachings, especially in retirement.

I retired from working on the national staff of the YMCA in 1980, at age sixty-five. My entire work life had been with the "Y." In fact, my connection to the "Y" goes back prior to my birth. My father was among a group of young, Japanese immigrant men in San Francisco who started a Japanese YMCA, in the basement of a Chinatown church, in the late nineteenth century. In the early 1900s, a man named Kyutaro Abiko bought land and established the Yamato Colony, a Japanese agricultural community in Livingston, California, which is in the San Joaquin Valley. A number of the men from the Japanese "Y," including my father, joined the colony. There were no women in the colony and the men sent to Japan for "picture brides." My mother was one of them and arrived in this country in 1912. Unfortunately, my father died when I was just seven years old and my mother was left with six young children, a forty-acre ranch to work and no command of English. We had seven terrible years and often went hungry. Mrs. Yona Abiko stepped in and rescued us and found a man for my mother to marry. He was a wonderful stepfather. We moved to San Francisco in 1929, I attended school in the city and graduated from the University of California, Berkeley.

My first job after graduation was at the Japanese branch of the San Francisco YMCA. Pearl Harbor occurred six months after I started working and the "Y" was padlocked a few months later. Not too long after that, my mother, stepfather, three brothers and I were all sent to a camp. That was in 1942 and I was twenty-seven years old at the time. The camps have been called internment camps but I call them concentration camps. They were family jails. Initially, my family was incarcerated at a former racetrack and all six of us lived in one small room, which had been a horse stall. The smell of horses penetrated everything. We were later sent to a camp in Topaz, Utah. I've blocked out a lot of the experience—I guess because I didn't want to remember. A professor at Cal State-Fullerton, told me a manuscript that I had written describing the camp experience was in the Bancroft library at U.C. Berkeley. I denied writing anything like that. When he showed it to me, I thought, this guy really knows how to write. I realized as I kept reading that no one else knew about that personal family stuff. I had to have written it.

I was able to get out of the camp early by applying, and being accepted to a YMCA college, Springfield College in Massachusetts. The college sponsored me and that was my ticket out. I received a master's degree there but then found it impossible to find a "Y" job because of my Japanese ancestry. I finally received an offer from the "Y" in Honolulu and immediately accepted it. I loved Hawaii and would have stayed there, but in 1947 I was

asked to reopen the Japanese "Y" in San Francisco and I felt obligated and returned (that concept of *Gi'ri*). I was there for ten years and during that time I changed it from a segregated branch to a community branch "Y." After that I headed up three other "Y" branches in the San Francisco area.

In 1968, I was offered a position on the YMCA national staff in Los Angeles and have been living here ever since. Among the programs I developed was NYPUM (National Youth Program Using Mini-Bikes), a program that eventually engaged 250,000 high-risk youth in productive activities. I never worried about how much money I made, as long as I could take care of my wife, Irene, and our two children, Bella and Matthew. We weren't rich in money but we were rich in spirit.

I had friends who became couch potatoes immediately after retirement and died not too long after. I knew I didn't want to become one of those couch potatoes. For ten years after my retirement, I did odds and ends, helping different YMCA branches by consulting, training and speaking. My volunteer work in the community eventually flowed from that and became a new career.

Today, despite my disabilities, I am able to contribute to the community. I can still talk, and by talking I can still influence and motivate people and help with fundraising efforts. I've been involved in helping four organizations in the Japanese-American community in Los Angeles: the Little Tokyo Service Center, the Japanese-American Community Service (JACS), the Japanese-American National Museum and the Japanese-American Citizens League.

The Little Tokyo Service Center provides a broad range of social services. At the very beginning, when I was invited on the Board, on which I still serve, the Center was essentially a one-man operation. It has expanded to such a degree that it now operates with an eight million dollars a year budget. JACS, another service organization, helps fund emerging social agencies and awards financial grants to community groups focusing on health, human services and cultural arts. I felt privileged when asked to join the Board and I've served on it for quite some time.

I played an important role in helping to raise funds for the building of the Japanese-American National Museum. I am a very effective fundraiser and I became one almost by accident as a result of meeting John Mott, the YMCA leader and 1946 Nobel Peace Prize winner. He received the prize for his role in establishing and strengthening Christian student organizations that worked to promote peace. He had a great influence on me and I thought of him as a mentor. He taught me not to directly ask for money when fundraising but to talk about the ideas, the dreams. He said the money would come if people thought the ideas were good and agreed with them. That's what I do; I talk about the visions, the dreams. It has worked for me, and in addition to the Museum, human service organizations have frequently asked me to help them raise money. I now teach others how to use this approach; you could say I'm now doing the mentoring. The idea is to multiply yourself through others.

The Museum, which opened in 1992, was the result of a ten-year-old dream shared by a number of people. It is the only museum in the United States dedicated to the experience of Americans of Japanese ancestry, and particularly to the Japanese-American experience during World War II. The museum now has an international reputation and it is a jewel. I was on the Board for many years and I now volunteer as a docent. I go every Thursday when I can, and I usually get a ride from one of the other volunteers.

My World War II experience motivated me to be on the Board of the local chapter of the Japanese-American Citizens League, which is the largest Asian civil rights organization in the country. I was a victim when I was put in a camp and as a result I try to do whatever I can to help others from being victimized. You can't be quiet, you must speak out. I believe the price of freedom is eternal vigilance.

I try to approach life in a holistic way; I think a combination of spirit, mind and body gives us the balance that we all need. I believe it is important to get and to stay involved and to look to the future. I think that has contributed to my longevity. Right now I'm looking forward to attending the one-hundredth anniversary of the Yamato Colony later this year.

Los Angeles, California

Fred Hoshiyama (b. 1914) and his wife, Irene, have been married fifty-nine years. Their son, Matthew, lives with them in their ranch house in Culver City. Matthew assists Fred, and helps with the care of Irene, who is ill. Bill Watanabe, the Executive Director of the Little Tokyo Service Center, describes Fred as "a very special and beloved person in our ethnic community."

5

Community-Based Art
and Service Programs
for Older Citizens

I was fortunate that my search for creative and productive older people led me to participants in two community-based art programs and one service program. I discovered that there are a number of such programs across the country committed to the development of creative and service potential in older citizens. These programs see creativity and service as being two of the keys or paths to healthy aging and the findings from preliminary research support this perspective; there is a positive connection between active participation in such programs and wellness.[1]

In 2006, the National Endowment for the Arts recognized fifteen model community-based art programs.[2] The individuals I interviewed are participants in two of the model programs: Elders Share the Arts in Brooklyn, New York, and the Burbank Senior Artists Colony in California. I interviewed three members of the Pearls of Wisdom, a touring ensemble of six elder storytellers sponsored by Elders Share the Arts, as well as a sculptor and a budding actress who are residents of the Burbank Senior Artists Colony.

The Pearls have been described as urban folk artists as they transform their personal memories and experiences into an oral art. Their personal stories are intertwined with American history and changes in our society; they give voice to history "from the ground up." They perform in a wide range of venues such as schools, libraries, settlement houses, correctional and drug treatment facilities and shelters for the homeless.

The Burbank Senior Artists Colony, the first of its kind, is a 141-unit senior apartment community in downtown Burbank. The colony is the brainchild of Tim Carpenter, the director of More than Shelter for Seniors, a non-profit organization providing housing for older citizens. The colony was designed for retired artists, musicians and entertainment industry professionals, as well as for individuals interested in pursuing the arts in their retirement. Numerous physical facilities are provided that support programs and classes in acting, dancing, creative writing and the visual arts.

The sixth person in this chapter is a member of the Experience Corps, a national tutoring program that was founded by Civic Ventures. Started in 1995, the Corps helps older Americans give back to their communities by being tutors and mentors in inner-city elementary schools. In 2007, the Corps operated in twenty cities and had over two thousand participating members. Independent research[3] has shown that the Experience Corps boosts the academic performance of students and helps schools become more successful. And similar to the community-based art programs, participation in the Corps enhances the well-being of its members.

1. Carrie Raiford
   Pearls of Wisdom Storyteller

2. Juliette Holmes
   Pearls of Wisdom Storyteller

3. Amatullah Saleem
   Pearls of Wisdom Storyteller

4. Gene Schklair
   Sculptor
   Burbank Senior Artists Colony Resident

5. Sally Spurgeon Connors
   Actress
   Burbank Senior Artists Colony Resident

6. Frank Nibley
   Experience Corps Tutor

Carrie Raiford
Age 84
Pearls of Wisdom Storyteller

In 1985, when I retired from working at a day-care center where I took care of young children, I was encouraged to join a senior citizens center. I didn't join at first because I didn't quite see myself going into a program with old people. My sister was going there and kept after me to join. One day, I decided to see what it was all about and spoke to the director, who told me about a program they had with Elders Share the Arts, with plays and art and storytelling. That sounded interesting to me. The Elders Share the Arts program was on Wednesdays, so I made it a point to go on that day as I enjoyed what they offered. One day, Peggy Pettie, from the program, had us sit in a circle and asked everyone to tell something they would have liked to have done in their life but hadn't known how to go about doing it. When she got to me I told her I would love to be a public speaker, to just stand before people and talk. She went around the group and when we had finished she said, "Well, I've found my storyteller. We are going to appoint Carrie Raiford as our storyteller."

That made me feel so good. I started telling living history stories, true stories about my life. My first story was about how I came up and I didn't leave anything out. I told about how my family was poor and lived on a farm as sharecroppers in South Carolina. My father and mother had nine children and we all worked hard picking cotton. My father was a man who really provided for his children and wanted all of us to go to school. He only finished the third grade and my mother finished fifth grade. All nine children ended up finishing high school and four went on to college.

I have about twelve stories I've been telling over the years. They are all in my head and I don't write them down, though they have been taped. Some of the most popular are: *How I Went to College, Back of the Bus* and *Ain't Nothing Changed.*

How I Went to College. I was the first in the family to go to college. My two older sisters didn't want to go. The eldest got married and the second one wanted to go to New York and start earning money. My second sister and I were in the same class in school. My father wasn't able to buy two sets of books so he went up to the school and told them to put me in the same class with my sister as I knew as much as she. And they did. My father decided I was the one who would go to college and my parents picked the college for me (Bettis Jr. College in Salutta, South Carolina). I kept wondering how on earth they could send me to college when they were sharecroppers and had no money. They drove to the college, made all the arrangements for me, and when they got back they told me I was accepted and not to worry.

When the day to leave arrived, I was told to pack my bags and get ready. My father said my mother couldn't come with us because he needed room in the car to load up stuff he had grown on the farm. When we got to the college, he drove around to the kitchen part of the school and unloaded all the stuff he had brought. After everything was unloaded they told him, "There is enough here to pay for one semester. You'll have to do the same thing again for the next semester." He had bartered his farm crops for my tuition! When my father was ready to leave, he took two quarters out of his pocket and said, "I want this to last you until you come home at Thanksgiving." And it did. I finished the two-year program in 1942 and received an Associates Degree. I then got a teaching job in a one-room schoolhouse, and got paid $50 a month. And that's how I got to college.

Back of the Bus. This was way before Rosa Parks. I came to New York one summer to work and earn some money and stayed with an aunt. That was in 1940 and I rode the New York City buses and sat wherever I wanted. I returned to South Carolina after the summer and decided to visit some friends. I took my five-year-old cousin with me and my father drove us to the bus stop. When I got on the bus, I absentmindedly sat in the front of the bus, three seats behind the driver. The bus filled up and I looked up and saw the bus driver staring at me. He ordered me to the back of the bus. I started trembling and I couldn't stop the trembling as I took my cousin and moved to the rear. I was afraid of what the bus driver would do to me and going through my mind were thoughts of being dragged into the woods and killed. I feared nobody would know what happened to me or be able to find me. When I was ready to get off, the driver turned on me and said, "Don't you ever try that again on my bus." I got off the bus crying and told my friends what had happened. I felt I couldn't return home on that bus and when it was time to go back, my friends had to drive me to meet my father. I expected my father to embrace me and tell me he was sorry when I told him what had happened. Instead he said, "But you know...you know better than that."

Ain't Nothing Changed. My husband and I got married in 1942 and he went into the Army and had to leave me. He was gone for three years and fought on the front lines. He experienced so much and saw so many friends shot down. After his discharge, we all waited at the train station for him and the other soldiers scheduled to arrive. The sheriff of this small town in South Carolina was also waiting for the train's arrival. When we saw him approach the soldiers, we thought he was going to welcome them back. He went up to them and said, "**Listen, boys,** I know you have been in the service, but I want to tell you one thing, **ain't nothing changed here.**" My husband later said to me, "I'm not taking this. I'm not going to let these people treat me like a dog after all I've been through. I'm going to New York." It was the middle of the school term for me and I joined him after the term was over. And that's the story of why we moved to New York City.

Life was different for us in New York. I couldn't get a teaching job here since I didn't have the credentials so I got into the day-care system. My husband worked as a chef in a restaurant. He died in 1979. Our two sons were born in New York and I now have five grandchildren and four great-grandchildren. I raised my eldest grandson and he lived with me until he went to Morehouse College. My one granddaughter is a graduate of Dartmouth College.

I'm a breast cancer survivor; I had a mastectomy in 1971, thirty-five years ago. I continue to see my cancer doctor every six months. I had a slight stroke five years ago but it did not leave me with any problems. I also fell and broke a hip and now have a plate in that hip. It doesn't bother me at all. I'm just plain blessed. I stay very busy; I walk every day for exercise, I'm occupied with my storytelling, keeping doctor's appointments, staying connected with my large family and with church activities. I'm a church-going lady and I go to church every Sunday. I belong to the Hebron Baptist Church and I love my church. I've been a member for a long time and I'm very active in it.

Storytelling is very important to me. I love it. There is nothing I enjoy better than going around and telling my stories. I don't ever get nervous. I've stood before three, four hundred people and don't feel nervous. It's not hard for me because it is what I want to do. Storytelling gives me something to do and to think about; I think about my life, about how I came up, what I've done, things that have happened to me, and that I'm eighty-four years old and living to tell it all. After I became a storyteller I thought about my father. He used to tell stories about his coming up; we would all sit together around the fireplace and listen to his stories. And here I am telling stories and getting paid for it!

Brooklyn, New York

Author's Note: A few days after our interview at the offices of Elders Share the Arts, I went to see Carrie perform in a civics class in a Bronx high school. I sat in the rear of the classroom as the students poured in at the start of the period. It had been a long time since I had been in a classroom with teenagers, and to me they seemed noisy, somewhat unruly, and I was aware of a lot of bantering and physical horseplay between the boys. I felt some concern for Carrie; she was, after all, eighty-four years old and at moments seemed physically frail. I wasn't sure how she would deal with this boisterous group. I needn't have worried. Once she began, the students fell silent and were absolutely spellbound; she held them in the palm of her hands. The class, many of whom were African-American and Hispanic, had been learning about segregation and the Jim Crow era in the south. Her personal stories were vivid and real and made history come alive, quite different from textbook learning. The students seemed to be profoundly affected and at the end of the period they spontaneously applauded. Many approached her after class to thank her and some of the girls hugged her.

Carrie was chosen to represent the Pearls of Wisdom at the United Nations' International Year of the Older Person and at the International Storytelling Conference in London. Her trip to London inspired her story, Lost in the System, *which is about the problems of getting a passport without a birth certificate. The midwife who delivered her in 1922 had not registered her birth. She eventually was able to get a belated birth certificate and regular passport.*

Juliette Holmes
Age - late 60s
Pearls of Wisdom Storyteller

I first heard about the Pearls from Carrie Raiford. A friend of mine has a theatre in her brownstone in Harlem and I attended a performance there. After the performance and during the dinner that followed, I had a delightful conversation with a woman, who turned out to be Carrie Raiford. During our conversation she said, "You would be a wonderful storyteller, I'd like you to join our group." She told me she was a professional storyteller and a member of the Pearls of Wisdom. She related how she had always wanted to be a public speaker; my own dream had been to be on the stage. Being in the South, my parents had frowned on that, as they knew the limits and barriers that existed at the time. Carrie gave me her card and the phone number for Elders Share the Arts. That was back in 2000 or 2001. I called and expressed my interest and left my number. I kept calling and checking in for two years before I was called for an interview. I had persisted because a seed had been planted and I could see myself as a storyteller.

I retired in 1995, after thirty-two years as an educator with the New York City Board of Education. At the time I met Carrie, I was an adjunct faculty member in the Continuing Education Program at the Bank Street College of Education. I was teaching a child development course to women who were moving from welfare to the work force and preparing for national certification in the Preschool Child Development Associate Credential Program.

I finally got a call and was interviewed by Thelma Thomas, the Artistic Director of the Pearls, who then invited me to join them. She explained that the stories would be about my own life and that I was expected to write them down. This all seemed doable as I like to write and I knew I had a lot of stories to tell. I met the other Pearls and over time we've bonded like a family. We meet once a month, listen to, and critique, one another's stories, and participate in workshops.

I used to write my stories on index cards and read them. I no longer need to read them when I perform. I now have ownership of my stories and when I present them it is like an out-of-body experience for me. I become so immersed in the stories, it is as if I'm floating but I'm still connected to the audience. I'm drawing them in so they can see and hear and feel what I'm describing.

One of my first stories, *Colored Water,* takes place in Savannah, Georgia, in 1950, before the enactment of civil rights laws. We couldn't drink from water fountains or use public facilities in those days. The story is about my experience as a little girl and my mother's act of courage in a Sears Roebuck Department store. As a result of her instruction and bravery in response to my thirst, I learned, much to my surprise, that "colored" water and "white" water, tasted the same. Another story, *Growing Up Geechee Gullah*, is about some of the traditions of the Geechee Gullah culture, told through the experience of the wonderful boat rides and picnic foods of my childhood. I love history and I do a lot of research that I bring into my stories. For instance, in the *Growing Up* story I tell that the Gullahs are of African slave ancestry, that they labored on the rice plantations, that the Gullah language is a distinctive English-African Creole that reflects significant influences from Sierra Leone, and that the Gullahs presently live in the coastal low country of South Carolina and Georgia. I merge my personal experiences and history together in my stories. I try to make them real and soulful. In addition, imbedded in the stories are values and principles I want to impart.

The two stories I'm working on now are about integrating Tybee Beach, a Savannah Beach, and about the first time my parents went to vote. We couldn't go to Tybee Beach when I was growing up. It was my dream to go there when I was a child, as it seemed like a place where people had so much fun. I recall my daddy taking us for a ride in the car one day and stopping and looking at Tybee Beach with its ice cream stands and amusement rides. A big cop came over to the car and said to my daddy, "Stop, boy, what are you doing down here? You know you people don't belong down here. This is only for white people. Now you just turn around." When the civil rights marches started, there were wade-ins to integrate the beaches. My daddy was one of the first people who drove the young people down to the wade-ins. There is a plaque honoring him for this in a museum in Savannah. So even if his children couldn't use the beach, he helped make it possible for his grandchildren and great-grandchildren.

In the story about my parents voting, I will include how my mother has a collection of peach stickers on her medicine cabinet mirror. Once when I went home to visit, I asked her, "Why do you have all these peaches on your mirror?" She explained, "Every time I brush my teeth or wash my face, I look at my peaches." The peach stickers are given out at the polls on Election Day and say, "I voted."

In 1976, I was awarded a fellowship from the African-American Institute and Columbia University's Teacher's College to travel and study in West Africa. We were required to choose an area of concentration and I chose African Art since I am a weaver. My African experience changed me. I saw people who looked like me and who looked like members of my family. They would say to me, "Welcome home, sister, welcome home, long time coming home." My soul connected; it was a powerful experience. It became my mission, when I got back, to teach as much as I could about what I had learned and continued to learn. I presented workshops at churches and developed a curriculum in African Studies and African Arts and Crafts for children in the New York City Public Schools. I'm hoping to go back to Africa soon and regain that connection. I want to experience it again now that I'm in a different stage of life.

I've had some medical problems in the past years. I could barely walk for a time due to arthritis in my knees and had two knee-replacement surgeries that were successful. I've also had glaucoma and underwent eye surgery. My eyes no longer allow me to do as much weaving and needlework as I once did. I used to exhibit my work and have won prizes, but I've given up much of that. Other things fill up that space now. My husband and I take care of our health by walking and watching what we eat. And I'm very active with my grandchildren. We also meditate and I have been doing so for over forty years. I'm a religious person and I pray over everything I do. I received strong values from my parents, which I try to live by, and to pass on to my son, grandchildren and friends. My husband and I are members of the Unity of Christianity Church.

I think being a Pearl opened a new adventure, a new experience in my life. I read somewhere, "Don't let your song die within you." That made an impression on me. I feel like I'm not letting my song die; I'm singing my song through words, through stories.

New York City

———————

Juliette Holmes was born and raised in Savannah, Georgia. She is a graduate of Savannah State College and received a Master's Degree from the Bank Street College of Education in New York. She has expertise in early childhood education. She and her husband, Cleveland, also an educator, met in college. He worked for the New York State Department of Mental Hygiene. They have lived in the same house in Queens for over forty years. They have one son, a "wonderful daughter-in-law" and two grandchildren. Juliette worked as a classroom teacher and in program and staff development in the New York City public schools. She was the recipient of the New York City Board of Education Teacher of the Year Award in 1986.

Amatullah Saleem
Age 75
Pearls of Wisdom Storyteller

I was an older student when I started taking courses at Empire State College. I'm one of those late bloomers. In college, I began writing stories and realized I loved writing. In my last term, one of my teachers told me that my stories were very interesting and wondered if I ever thought about storytelling. She suggested I do my internship at Elders Share the Arts and she made an appointment for me. During my internship at ESTA, I became more and more interested in watching the Pearls tell their personal stories. Carrie Raiford and Roberta Jones encouraged me to tell mine and they gave me much warmth and support, which I appreciated. I eventually became a member of the Pearls.

I've been a member for four years and I now have a repertoire of ten stories. I write all my stories first and then memorize them. I sometimes rewrite a story a number of times before I consider it finished. Other aspects sometimes come to me while I'm performing. I may add things or change the shape of a story depending on audience reaction. Even when I'm not actually sitting down and writing, I may be thinking about a story for a long time.

The popularity of certain stories seems to change over time. Right now, the story I am asked to tell most often is *Sister Barbara 21X,* about how I became a Muslim. Changing one's religion is a process; it takes a long time, as it is a very important decision. I joined the Nation of Islam in the 1970s. I know the teachings of Elijah Muhammad were quite controversial at the time. His teachings, which I found helpful, were specifically for black

197

Americans who were having problems and they were tailored to help us improve our lives. He dealt not only with the external enemy (the white man) but also with the self-hatred we carried from slavery. The Nation of Islam is now moving more and more in the direction of mainstream Islam. Our practices were initially very restrictive; we didn't go to movies or socialize outside of our mosques and the clothes we wore were very modest. That has changed. We now read the Holy Koran, which we did not do initially, and I hope one day I can afford to make the pilgrimage to Mecca.

I have stories about different stages of my life. I grew up in the south and some of my stories are about my family's migration to the north. They moved to find work, to have a better life, a better education for their children and to escape the segregation and racism of the time. My first story was about my grandmother who raised me. I initially told that one a lot. I think it was because I was only telling stories to children back then. My other stories have appealed to teenagers and adults.

I moved to Washington, D.C., with my grandmother when I was seven years old and then, when my mother married, I moved to join her and my stepfather in Brooklyn. I was a teenager in New York City during the jazz age. I had the opportunity and pleasure of hearing people like Miles Davis, Charlie Parker, JJ Johnson and John Coltrane. They were struggling musicians at the time and had not yet become famous. They would come to little clubs in Brooklyn and my friends and I would dance to their music. One of my stories is about John Coltrane. People can relate to these stories because they are a part of the history of jazz.

I also have stories about becoming a dancer and about traveling in Europe as an African-American artist. I always loved to dance when I was growing up. It was an important part of being black; we would dance to blues, rhythm and blues, and jazz. When I moved to New York I saw the movie *Cabin in the Sky*. The movie made me realize for the first time that dancing could be a career.

While in high school, I accompanied a friend who had to take a little girl to her dance class in Manhattan on 43rd Street. Her class was at the Katherine Dunham Dance School and I found it to be a fascinating place.

When we went upstairs it seemed to me as if the walls were shaking with the drumming and that the pictures of the company in their costumes were pulsating. I was hooked after that and knew that I wanted to be a dancer. I spoke to the registrar, got accepted, and worked and saved money for classes. I studied dance there for three years after graduating from high school, and then became a member of the company.

Dance company members who had toured Europe came back with exciting tales. I was tired of the racism in this country and two friends and I decided to save money and take off for Europe. I ended up staying in Europe for ten years. While there, I danced with the Katherine Dunham Company on tour until the company disbanded. I then became part of a duo with a male dancer from Santiago, Cuba, and we worked in nightclubs, casinos and theatres for three years.

I became pregnant while in Amsterdam. I had grown tired of traveling and of the nightclub scene and I wanted my baby to have a more stable life. So I returned to New York City where my daughter was born. She is deaf so I had the experience of raising a deaf child. It was exciting to be back in the country in the 1960s as it was the time of the civil rights movement. I taught at a dance studio that I started in SoHo (before it was called SoHo). I closed it when I received a job offer to be a dance/music specialist in Winston-Salem, North Carolina. I stayed there for fifteen years and moved back to New York when I realized my mother was ill and needed my help. She died five years after my return. I was glad we had time to resolve the issues between us.

I worked in various jobs once I was back in New York, including one as a recreational dance teacher and another as an administrative secretary. I struggled to teach myself computer skills while in the last job and at some point decided I needed to get a college education. I eventually received a B.S. Degree in Dance Studies from Empire State College and after that I joined the Pearls.

My life is very busy at the present time. In addition to storytelling, I have obligations at the mosque and I teach physical movement classes to senior citizens three times a week. I'm active in two organizations: Harlem

LOC (Local Organizing Committee of Harlem), an organization dedicated to identifying and working on community problems; and Black New Yorkers for Educational Excellence, an organization working to improve education for black children in the school system. I'd like to have more time for story writing and I'd like to go back to college at some point and take more creative writing classes. I'm also interested in getting a Master's Degree in Folklore. My daughter, Opal, who is now forty years old, is presently undergoing treatment for breast cancer and I try, as much as possible, to be available to her and to my seven-year-old granddaughter, Osirah.

My health is good although I don't have the strength I used to have and I no longer can take my health for granted. I have arthritis and osteoporosis and I need to exercise regularly or I really feel the consequences. I exercise when I teach but it isn't enough for me so I also take Pilates for seniors, and Katherine Dunham Technique classes.

It is a blessing for me to be a Pearl. It has been a lifesaver. My life as a professional dancer had to come to an end. I am fortunate that I could take the creative energy I used in dance and transfer it to a new medium. I've been able to make use of my stage experience and apply it to storytelling. There are similarities between the two; in both dance and storytelling you need to project, to communicate, to memorize your piece, and to wear a costume. One difference for me is the use of my voice, which I've needed to work on. I try to use movement in my storytelling. I've performed two one-woman shows, one a couple of years ago and one last year for Elders Share the Arts at the Whitney Museum of American Art in New York City. In both of them I combined dance movement and storytelling. I'm still developing and growing as a storyteller. It is an art form and I still have a lot to learn.

New York City

Amatullah Saleem (b. 1931) lives in a Manhattan apartment with her daughter and granddaughter. In addition to her numerous activities, she wrote and produced a children's musical, A Reflection of the Harlem Renaissance, *for elementary school students at the Muhammad University of Islam. In May 2005, Amatullah was the representative spokesperson for Elders Share the Arts at the White House Mini Conference on Creative Aging. Her testimony on the vital issues of creativity throughout her life reflected her devotion and evolution as an artist and teacher.*

Gene Schklair
Age 76
Sculptor
Burbank Senior Artists Colony Resident

I have made myself over, or reinvented myself, four times. First I was a manager of a women's clothing store, next a dental surgeon, then a trekker, and now a full-time sculptor.

I've been sculpting, on and off, all my life. In fact, my earliest memory is of working with a piece of clay at age four. It turns out that there have been artists on both sides of my family going back many generations, so I think it is in my genes. My father, a carpenter, didn't approve of art as a career and he wouldn't support my aspirations of going to art school, which is a shame. So I went into the service right after high school. I had no higher education when Glorya and I married in 1952. We came from very different types of families; hers, in contrast to mine, was warm, genteel and well educated.

In 1955, I was managing a women's wear store and Glorya and I decided I was getting nowhere. Upon her urging, we made a decision that she would support me and I would go back to school. We had to find a career for me and decided on the health field. I chose dentistry rather than medicine, which would have taken too long, especially since we already had one child. I received my undergraduate and dental school degrees from the University of Illinois in Chicago. Glorya worked nights the years I was in school, and by the time I received my D.D.S., we had three children and the fourth was on the way.

Dentistry was a wise choice for me and cosmetic dentistry became my art form. I was innovative and I was one of the dentists who pioneered dental implants; there were probably only one hundred dentists in the country, maybe the world, doing them in the late 1960s. My practice eventually became very successful and we had a lovely custom-made home built for us in a Chicago suburb. And then I got sick.

I started having asthma attacks in 1972 but they were manageable. By 1983, my whole immune system had collapsed. I had many episodes when I would stop breathing and had to be rushed to the hospital and be given emergency drugs. I would feel better, go back to work, and then have another episode. Nobody knew what was wrong or put those two things together. No one knew about industrial allergies in those days. Both an immunologist and my internist told me I would probably die within the year. I was fifty-four at the time and at the peak of my career. I felt the rug had been pulled out from under me. I had to sell my practice; something I loved and still miss. I started feeling better away from the office but I was still fragile and weak and I could not breathe without heavy doses of cortisone.

Glorya suggested that, instead of sitting around waiting for me to die, we plan a trip—a backpacking trip—around the world. She convinced me and we bought travel books, went to a travel agent, acquired two large backpacks and prepared for our journey. Glorya closed her business, we sold our house and our cars; we liquidated everything we had worked so hard to build. At first our kids were very upset about our plans and then eventually said, "Go for it." We figured I would die somewhere along the way. I had this image that we would walk into the sunset together, hand in hand, and then she would bring me back in a box.

We started off going to Asia and chasing the sun. I had good days and bad days. The bad days were usually in countries with high pollution. On the good days you would never know I was ill except I had a moon face from cortisone. Cortisone kept me alive but the long-term use was destructive to my teeth and bones. We visited twenty-six countries in ten months. We

had a glorious trip and everywhere we went we made friends, some are still friends to this day. And I was still alive when we returned to Chicago!

We decided to move to California where three of our children lived. So we picked up our daughter, Vicki, who is challenged due to brain damage she suffered as a child, and drove west. Glorya resumed her career as a professional organizer and started working for small businesses and home entrepreneurs. I began consulting with a holistic medical practitioner who had a Ph.D. in biochemistry and was interested in my type of problem. He tested me for allergens and peeled me like an onion searching for the big allergen that was the root problem. It turned out to be self-curing acrylic. Liquid acrylic is a very toxic substance and I had used it in making temporary teeth. Dentists didn't wear masks back in those days, and I had been inhaling acrylic for years. We embarked upon a course of treatment, which involved injecting me with as much of the allergen as I could tolerate at a time. The amounts were gradually increased with the goal of eventually reducing my sensitivity. It worked and, after eighteen months of shots, I was cured. Facing death, and getting my life back, makes me appreciate the life I have. I don't take it for granted. I look in the mirror every morning and grin and say, "I'm here."

Around the time I was getting better, our daughter, Vicki, was attending a school to learn self-sufficiency skills. A group of parents and I got together to make papier-mâché sculptures and other decorations in preparation for one of the school's fundraising events. That's when the itch to do sculpture started up again. I had previously worked with clay and lost wax and this time I began doing large, papier-mâché pieces. I found that I didn't like the medium because it takes so long to dry. So I began experimenting with plaster-impregnated orthopedic gauze. Oh boy, it set in only four minutes. I loved it and I've been using it ever since. The way I now work is to create a wire armature and cover it with layers of large wet strips of plaster-impregnated gauze. I then add small pieces for the details, like the fingers and facial features.

Around twenty years ago, I finally was able to start seriously devoting myself to sculpture. I am self-taught and it took me a long time to get it right. My sculptures of people are life size. I love doing pieces that have humor and whimsy. Very often the pieces have two levels of meaning; in addition to the humor there is a deeper intellectual message about the human condition. Glorya has asked me why I make such large pieces since transporting them is so difficult. I have to make what I feel. When I really *feel* what I'm doing, it comes out right. I believe my soul goes into the good ones. Sometimes I have so many pieces going on in my head at the same time, I have to work on them simultaneously. Over the years, I've exhibited my work in numerous galleries, as well as in juried shows and art fairs. At one show in Beverly Hills, I sold all the pieces before the end of the first day; one was sold right off the tailgate.

Glorya and I were among the first people to move in here (the Burbank Senior Artists Colony) when it opened in May 2005. She had read an article in the L.A. *Times* about Tim Carpenter (the director) and his plans for the Colony. We got very excited, particularly because a sculpture studio was planned. We had been feeling the strain of keeping up a house and had talked about moving into a condo. My studio was in the garage and I would have been without a studio if we moved into a condo. Glorya says I would die if I couldn't do my sculpture. So moving here was an exciting solution.

Glorya has copies of the letters she wrote to family members during our trek, and at an earlier time had attempted to write a book based on the letters. Being here has inspired her to resume writing and finish the book, and she has gotten much encouragement from others. It is now pouring out of her. She is calling it, *Travels with a Dead Man*, and describes it as a combination love story, a coping with death story, and a travel story.

I always like to tell how I see people moving in here who have given up on life. You look at their eyes and their eyes are dead. Within a month, they become active and excited about living. Life is vibrant here. Glorya and I are very involved in this community. I'm President of the Residents' Council and she leads a current events discussion group that she started, which meets every Friday after the yoga class. There are about seventy of us who get together often and have become very good friends. It has been wonderful forming these friendships at this stage in our lives. These friends, in addition to our four children and two granddaughters, who all live in Los Angeles, are now the important people in our lives. This is our community. This is our home.

Burbank, California

(Special thanks to Glorya Schklair for her contributions.)

Author's note: Gene was waiting for me at the front door of the apartment building at our agreed-upon appointment time. Also greeting me, next to the door in the lobby, was a life-size sculpture. The sculpture is of an old woman holding a door partially open, as if for a visitor. As I looked through that door, I was startled to see myself, the visitor, reflected in a full-length mirror. This was one of several of Gene's sculptures exhibited in the large lobby. As he took me on a tour of the building, I was able to see more of his work in the sculpture studio, as well as in his apartment. Many have the combined quality of whimsy and serious commentary that he mentions.

Both Gene and Glorya are warm, friendly, lively and loquacious people and they immediately made me welcome. I could see how they so easily made friends when they traveled. They are very affectionate with one another and it was moving to me when Glorya, in reference to Gene, said, "I can still see the eighteen-year-old kid and he was gorgeous. And I hope that's the way he sees me." In addition to being a "love story, a coping with death story and a travel story," I found their story to also be one of courage and the triumph of spirit in the face of adversity. It felt natural when we all hugged one another when we parted.

Sally Spurgeon Connors
Age 75
Actress
Burbank Senior Artists Colony Resident

I assumed my life in retirement would continue to be the same-old, same-old. My husband and I would remain in the same house in Chicago, which we didn't like, and were always planning to sell or fix up, but never did. I would continue to work on genealogy, which was an interest of mine, and spend a lot of time in the basement. My computer was in the basement as was my stash of food. Nobody could see me eating in the basement where I went to soothe myself by eating. That's how I envisioned my retirement years. I also thought I would be the first to die as my husband was sure he would live to one hundred twenty. I never dreamed of the life I have now. I never knew I had it in me.

My husband died two-and-a-half years ago at age seventy-eight. We had a long marriage of forty-six years, but it was a very bad marriage. No, I shouldn't say that, it was not a particularly good marriage. Before he died, he suffered from a type of dementia, which seemed to have come on suddenly. His doctor diagnosed him as having an underlying schizophrenic-paranoid syndrome. That helped me understand some of his past behavior. I had tolerated a lot throughout the years, as had our two daughters. But that's all water over the dam. I consider myself a survivor as I had two alcoholic parents as well as an alcoholic husband. I think I deserve all the great stuff I'm getting now; I certainly worked hard enough for it.

After my husband's death I decided to sell the house and initially planned to spend six months of the year in Champaign-Urbana, where my daughter, Cheryl, and her husband and three children live, and the other six months in or around Glendale, California, near my daughter, Liz. I came out to Glendale to find a place to live and nothing looked particularly good to me. Liz said that while driving around, she saw a place she thought would be wonderful for me, the Burbank Senior Artist Colony. I said, "Why should I go to an artist colony? I haven't done anything artistic in my entire life." She responded, "You have it in you. I think you should be here and I think you would really enjoy it." So I made an appointment with Rose, who works in the office here. Even before I saw the available apartment, I saw the activities sheet for the month. Oh, my goodness.

I'm funny; I'm religious and not religious and superstitious and not superstitious. I had to make a quick decision about reserving the apartment and needed a certified check to do so. There was a Catholic church near the bank where I could draw the check and I said to myself, "If the church is open and I can go in, it will be a sign that I should take the apartment." Lo and behold, the door was open. I walked in, said a few prayers, and then went to the bank and got my check. That's how I got to be here. I moved in with just two suitcases of clothes. I made a break with the past and started a new life.

Once I moved here, I joined almost every activity group offered. I joined the acting group, the chorus, the creative writing group and the painting group. I came here in October, a year and a half ago, and the acting group was already working on a Christmas show, *Christmas Eve in Malibu*. I asked if it was too late for me to join. The group said no, they had written the play themselves and would write in a part for me.

This was my first time on stage since being in high school plays. In retrospect, I do think my experience as a junior high school science teacher was good preparation. I was a very good teacher and was forever working to engage my students. I honed my craft in front of a very critical audience.

At performance time I was scared to death. Barbara, our drama coach and director, took me aside and said, "Remember this, you are giving a gift to the audience and you want to give them the best that you can." Once I

got out on stage, the audience laughed at my lines and I thought, "I'm not only giving them a gift, look at the gift they are giving back to me. They think I'm funny." I had a ball. It was the highest high I've ever had. I've never done drugs so I don't know what that's like but I experienced a real high. And everyone told me afterwards how good I was. I've had a part in all the plays we have performed here since then. I love acting, it is an exhilarating experience and it continues to be a high.

A relatively new resident, Jack Nicholson (not the famous actor), who directed shows in Las Vegas, recently directed three one-act plays here. I had a part in one of them, *The Happy Journey* by Thornton Wilder. Jack is a professional; he worked us very hard and taught me so much. He coached me to get in character and stay in character. When we were finished with the play, I experienced a low for a week as I had been so immersed in the play and it was hard to let go.

I've recently been cast in a film called *The Pursuit of Loneliness*. Laurence Thrush, an independent filmmaker is the screenwriter, director and producer. He plans to show the movie at film festivals and is looking for a distributor. It is a film about how the city of Los Angeles, following the death of an old lady who has been all alone, handles her burial and property. I play the old lady. Mr. Thrush came to our building two months ago looking for someone to play the part. He had apparently visited all the senior buildings in the area. Out of the blue, he called me up and told me I was the best person for the role and he wanted me in the film. I have the screenplay and I'm learning the part, which is quite long. We start filming this summer and I'm very excited.

I've also had an opportunity to perform with the chorus, which gives a number of performances here at our theater complex and at other residences. I love to sing and sing all the time. When I was in high school, I wanted to be a singer with a band. That dream lasted for about a year and then I decided teaching was a more practical and realistic career for me. At one of our concerts, I was the soloist with a combo and sang two songs, *Sentimental Journey* and *Blue Moon*. I was so scared beforehand I thought I would throw up. But it turned out to be a lot of fun and I was very well received. My daughter, Liz, was in the audience and said she knew I was good but hadn't realized how good. I never thought that dream of being a soloist in front of an audience would become a reality.

I've also been participating in a type of mentorship project called the CDS/Art Colony Project. Ten of us from the Colony are paired with ten students from the neighboring Community Day School, an alternative school for students who were having a hard time making it in regular junior and senior high schools. We meet regularly with the students and have different scheduled activities. These have included sharing with one another the negative perceptions and stereotypes we feel society has of older people and of teenagers who need to be in an alternative school. We have worked on masks of how we think people view us and we are getting ready to jointly paint a mural with signs and symbols of how we see our lives. We talk together about time lines and future plans. The teen I was paired with never before had an adult express interest in his dreams or hopes beyond high school. Since our discussions, he has begun to formulate a plan for his future. The school principal has told us that the students look forward to our visits. We don't see the results of our contacts but she does.

I go to yoga class here every Monday and Friday morning and an anti-aging exercise class every Tuesday and Thursday, where we do strength and flexibility training. I've gotten stronger and can do many physical things I couldn't do before I came here. My knees and back, where I have arthritis, feel much better. I've always had a weight problem and I now eat better and have lost thirty pounds. I've become very active in the social life of the community. I see a psychotherapist once a week and that has been enormously helpful. I had a lot of self-worth issues and therapy and my life here have contributed to an increase in my self-esteem.

I had initially planned to spend six months here in California and six months in Champaign-Urbana. After just three months at the Colony, I knew I didn't want to leave. I was so relieved and thankful when Cheryl said she thought I had a good life here and should stay put. I now go back to Illinois for visits with Cheryl and her family and to see my older brother and friends.

I have such a full life now; I am so happy and love it here. I'm drawing on so many parts of myself I never realized were there. I guess it takes courage and the willingness to take a chance.

Burbank, California

Frank Nibley
Age 73
Experience Corps Tutor

I envisioned retirement as a time to play golf, do lots of deep-sea fishing and live the life of Riley, if I could possibly afford it. I was a bank vice president and in 1996, at age sixty-two, I took early retirement from the First Hawaiian Bank, where I had worked for almost forty years. I had spent close to six of those years on the Big Island of Hawaii as a regional vice president, supervising the bank's branches. I thought we might retire on the west coast of the Big Island because Honolulu, where we lived, had become extremely congested. But as it turned out, our plans changed and we moved here to Tucson instead.

Two or three years before my retirement, my wife, Diane, joined her sister on a genealogical trek across the country, tracking down their older relatives in order to fill in the blanks in their family tree. Arizona was one of the states they passed through and she called me to tell me that it was a beautiful state and we should consider it as a possible retirement spot. After two or three trips here I was sold, and we bought a lot and built a house on the first fairway in a Del Webb development. In keeping with my retirement vision, one of the very first things I did was go out and purchase a golf cart.

I knew at the time that I didn't want to become involved with boards of directors or be on committees or do volunteer work. I had devoted so much of my time to those activities over so many years in banking and I needed a break. When I first started working at the bank there were three hundred employees and by the time I retired the number had grown to two

215

thousand. I can't even tell you how many branches there were by that time. It was like a roller coaster all of the time I was there—growth, growth, growth. Statehood for Hawaii was the real driver in spurring that growth over the years. So I was tired and ready for a change.

Along with golf and leisure, good health had been part of my retirement vision and that changed eight years ago. In 1999, I was afflicted with cancer—very serious, stage four, neck and throat cancer. That put the brakes on my dream and put me out of commission for a number of years. I guess things changed in my own mind during that time. I felt I had enjoyed a great life and perhaps I could give something back.

A little over two years ago, Diane drew my attention to a full-page article in a newspaper supplement about the Experience Corps. They were conducting an informational meeting at one of the public libraries and she thought I might be interested. I somewhat reluctantly agreed to go and she went along with me. I signed up that very day and have been with the Experience Corps ever since. It has become my way of giving back.

My health is presently stable and I am monitored very closely. The doctors are still trying to figure out what happened. I incurred a lot of residual damage from the treatment. My speech was affected, necessitating a considerable amount of speech therapy. It turns out that reading with the children has been very therapeutic for me.

I did not have any prior experience teaching academic subjects to young children although I had done other types of teaching. I was a professional ballroom dancer before I started my career in banking and for six years I was an instructor in the Arthur Murray system. A one-year contract instructing dance teachers was responsible for my move to Hawaii from my home base on the West Coast. In addition to teaching in the dance world, I later assisted in teaching finance courses at the University of Hawaii, where I had completed my studies in Business Administration.

Both the initial and ongoing training provided by the Corps has been very helpful. There are presently three Experience Corps tutors at this school and we anticipate seven more joining us. We primarily work on reading skills, although we also help the children with spelling, writing and math when needed. I put a good deal of effort into writing each child's

monthly progress report so that the teachers know exactly what I am doing and we can coordinate learning goals.

The core of my week, Tuesday, Wednesday and Thursday, is devoted to tutoring. I get up at four a.m. on those days and leave the house a little before six. It takes me an hour to drive from my home to the school, the Centennial Elementary School in the Flowing Wells District in Tucson. I start the day here in the teachers' lounge where I work out my game plan for the day. I tutor seven students, thirty minutes each, three times a week. They range from kindergartners to fifth graders.

The children I tutor tend to come from underprivileged backgrounds, they are low achievers and sometimes are English learners. Many of the families have problems that make it difficult for them to provide these students with the time and attention children require. I find I must totally focus on each child and what that child needs in order to be effective; the child sets the agenda. These children need attention, they need to bond and they need love. I try to provide them with the experience of being with an adult who cares about them, is committed to their well-being and their learning. I take this job very seriously. The children let me know that I am missed when I am not here; I am an important presence in their lives. The teachers corroborate that.

Tutoring the children is the central part of my week. I don't get in much golf or fishing anymore but I do get to swim every day. The rest of my week is organized around spending time with my wife, going to movies, doctor's appointments, doing errands, going to church, visiting friends, and keeping in contact with my friends in Hawaii and with my family. I also like to write, particularly poetry. I recently submitted a short piece about tutoring one of the children to the *Reader's Digest.*

Although I went to Mass faithfully every Sunday before I became ill, religion wasn't as integral a part of my life as it is now. My faith was renewed and I started taking it more seriously once I became ill. At one point I was going to church daily. I now go to seven a.m. Mass every Sunday and I find being in church fulfilling and enriching. I use Sunday mornings as a time to reflect, give thanks, and pray.

I have had a great life and I've seen and done so much. I raised three sons on my own after my first wife and I divorced and I'm very proud of them. They are all doing well, they are married, and I have six grandchildren with the seventh on the way. Diane and I have now been married for thirty years. We dated in high school and reconnected many years later after she took a trip to Hawaii and mutual friends gave her my address and suggested she look me up.

Over the years, I've been involved in the political arena in Washington and worked with many politicians, Senator Daniel Inouye among them. I've traveled the world, met so many interesting people and served on any number of boards of directors, including the Western Pacific Regional Fishery Management Council, which regulates fishing in federal waters. There isn't much I've missed. I've made every minute count.

The modest stipend I receive from the Experience Corps didn't influence my decision to enlist in the Corps. The driving is long and the work is time consuming, but as long as I am making a contribution it is worthwhile to me. It is a marvelous, gratifying experience. Hopefully, I can keep doing it. I have no plans of taking early retirement from this job.

Tucson, Arizona

Author's Note: I interviewed Frank at the school the day before Halloween. He had gotten up even earlier than usual to pick up Halloween cookies for the students. The children call him "Mr. Frank" and that morning his nametag read "Mr. Frankenstein." Briea, an eight-year-old girl he tutors, had jokingly nicknamed him that because of his height; he is a tall man (six feet, two inches), and he towers over the younger children. His height accentuated the difficult working conditions with which he must cope—child-size tables and chairs set up in the hallway. The chairs are cramped and uncomfortable for adults and the hallway is a source of distraction for the children.

I met three of the students Frank tutors. His manner with them was caring and gentle; the children were very relaxed with him and the bond with each one was apparent. Frank is highly valued by the school personnel and both the principal, Dr. Lynette Patton, and one of the teachers sought me out in the teachers' lounge to let me know how much they appreciated him. Ms. Gowler, a second grade teacher, speaking of Frank said, "He has worked with some of my most difficult students. He is a man of great patience and creativity who always tries to figure out what will work best with the children. He has been a great asset to me as a classroom teacher." Dr. Patton added that she thought one of the reasons the school's Experience Corps was known as one of the better programs was because of Frank's leadership. As a result of the program's reputation, the school has hosted numerous national and state visitors who are interested in the Experience Corps.

6

Living Longer and Better

I found the people whose stories you have been reading inspiring and sometimes amazing. In this chapter, I've pulled together what I see as the characteristics and themes shared by this diverse set of people. I believe they have much to teach us about living engaged, productive and creative lives.

Passion, Commitment, Meaningfulness

One of the things that impressed me, over and over again, was the passion and commitment the individuals I interviewed felt for the activities in which they were engaged. They saw their endeavors as being important and meaningful, as well as adding excitement and zest to their lives. They were not doing busy work. They felt their overall sense of well-being was enhanced by their creative activities, and two of the artists, ages ninety-four and ninety-five, thought their creative lifestyle contributed to their longevity. Here are just a few examples taken from the stories.

Art has become such an important part of my life; it is a blessing to be able to do it. I get such a high out of the creative process.

Sheldon Markel

I taught for forty years and I loved being a classroom teacher but I think the Family Learning Institute is the best thing I've ever done. We are taking children destined to a life of failure and turning their lives around.

Doris Sperling

It has been a rich experience for me to help people be creative and bring joy into their lives. I think when you give, you receive back many times over.

Carrie Lo

Working on cars keeps me interested in life. I love knowing how machines operate and I love solving the puzzles and finding the solutions when machines aren't operating properly. Every morning I look forward to working on a car, figuring out why something doesn't work and how to fix it.

Raymond Nelson

It is gratifying to me when I help others muster their strengths and abilities and I can assist them in finding hope. It is also satisfying when I teach Stephen Ministry volunteers new skills that they can use in the helping process.

Carleen McGinn

I still feel emotional excitement about my work and look forward to each day and the joy of creation. I think my longevity and good health are due to the good genes I inherited from my parents but also from the physical energy I derive from the way I live.

Harry Steinberg

Preconditions

In addition to sharing a passion or commitment for their respective endeavors, those interviewed, with very few exceptions, had five features or characteristics in common, which appear to be preconditions for creative aging. These conditions did not ensure creativity but they did provide the foundation that made it possible. These include financial security, freedom from a full-time caregiving role, emotional ties and involvement with others, and the maintenance of both cognitive and physical functioning. The latter three features are consistent with the characteristics identified as contributing to "successful aging," in Rowe and Kahn's book,[1] mentioned in chapter two.

Financial Security

The financial circumstances differed greatly among the participants but all had adequate or sufficient resources to support themselves. Some combination of social security, pensions, annuities, savings and investments, part-time employment, as well as subsidized or rent-controlled housing, made this possible. No one was in a situation that necessitated full-time employment due to financial need. Such a condition would have made the pursuit of creative activities difficult, as time and energy would have been in short supply. Some individuals chose to continue in their jobs on a limited basis after their official retirement and a number of the participants pursued part-time or full-time second careers, which satisfied their desire for creative or productive endeavors, and for which they received an income.

Freedom from a Full-time Caregiving Role

No one in this group of thirty-seven was presently a full-time caregiver of a seriously ill or severely disabled relative. Situations of that kind are very demanding and caregivers have little time and energy left for themselves, much less for creative pursuits. One woman I interviewed, an artist whose story is not included in the book, took care of a seriously ill husband for many years. It was a full-time job and only after his death was she able to return to her painting.

Social Relationships

A considerable body of social science research indicates that emotional and social connectedness promotes both mental and physical well-being and contributes to longevity. Strong emotional ties and social connections to others were evident among this group; no one was socially isolated. They were involved in relationships and networks in which they contributed, as well as received, emotional support and assistance. Family connections were primary and the relationship with spouse was the most important and meaningful for married individuals. All the men in this group had wives and felt fortunate that their wives were alive and most were in relatively good health. One man's wife was in the early stages of Alzheimer's disease and the couple was receiving support and assistance from their family and community. Another man had a seriously ill wife and he was receiving help with her care from a family member. In contrast to the men, slightly more than half of the women were single, divorced or widowed. Close relationships with family members and friends compensated for the absence of a partner. In addition to family and friends, social networks and support systems included affiliation and involvement with a church, synagogue, or mosque, as well as professional and service organizations and interest groups.

Maintenance of Cognitive or Mental Functioning

Interviewees recognized that aging affected their speed of learning as well as their memory. They did, however, think that their productive pursuits, physical exercise, stimulation from their social network, and learning and mastering new skills and information contributed to the maintenance of complex cognitive processes. College-level classes, law courses taken on-line, learning to create web sites, doing crossword puzzles, reading, and a weekly "lunch bunch" to discuss politics are just a few of the many examples of ongoing learning and mental challenges mentioned in the narratives.

Maintaining Physical Functioning

No one was free from physical problems and all recognized that these, like the cognitive changes, were inevitable realities of aging. Energy levels varied, not only because of age differences; some were just higher energy people than others. Everyone had awareness of declining stamina and energy. What stood out were the adaptations they made, as well as the effort and discipline they devoted to maintaining their physical health and fitness. The most frequently mentioned physical problems were arthritis (many had received hip or knee replacements), osteoporosis, hearing loss and decline in vision. Additional serious health concerns included cancers that were in remission, cardiac problems, and fibromyalgia. None of them let their physical problems keep them from functioning. In fact, two individuals sought meaningful service activities after bouts with cancer.

There were numerous adaptations to losses in functioning as well as some positive reversals of medical problems. For example, Molly Agras, in an effort to alleviate debilitating and painful rheumatism, embarked upon a disciplined regimen of yoga and swimming. She thinks that it made a big difference in her physical aging and kept her rheumatism in check. As a result of her improved physical condition, she was able to start a new freelance interior design business in her sixties. Marvin Nochman's hearing loss made it difficult for him to pick up entry cues when performing in plays. Rather than give up theatre work, which would have been a great loss to him, he enlisted the help of crewmembers to signal the cues he could not hear. Thus far he has been able to manage with that assistance. Carrie Lo, after an elbow replacement, was no longer able to do detailed flower painting. She started employing a freer brush stroke as well as painting more landscapes. As a consequence, she has become more courageous and experimental in her artwork and is pleased with the change.

Those interviewed were committed to a healthy lifestyle and were knowledgeable about what that involved—nutritious diet, lack of destructive habits, appropriate health care and exercise to stay fit. Regular and disciplined physical exercise was important in the lives of most of those interviewed and most attributed physical and cognitive benefits to their exercise regimens.[2]

Although maintaining physical functioning is a precondition of great importance, exceptions do exist. There are some exceptional older people who are involved in creative activities *despite* physical disabilities or chronic illnesses. For example, Jai-Zhen Song, during years of serious illness and incapacity, was able to compose an important body of music. In his post-retirement career, Fred Hoshiyama, who is legally blind and very hard of hearing, is still able to give inspirational talks and be an effective fundraiser.

Approaching Mortality: Religion and Spirituality

Age, along with retirement, with its increase in available time and decreasing responsibilities, contributes to a heightened awareness of one's mortality and the passage of time. This, in turn, can foster a reevaluation of beliefs, values and priorities. It was interesting to find that the meaning and role of religion and spirituality varied greatly among those interviewed. A few individuals, as they grew older, sought deeper religious paths. Many described their religious beliefs and religious affiliations as the crucial, central aspect of their lives, contributing to their overall sense of well-being. Others indicated that they maintained church or synagogue affiliation primarily for the social support or sense of community it provided. Some held religious beliefs but did not choose to belong to any religious organization. Approximately one-fifth of those interviewed identified themselves as atheists or skeptics.

Joseph Chuman, Ph.D., a prominent Ethical Culture leader and faculty member at Columbia University, offers two definitions of spirituality.[3] The first, and more traditional one, involves a belief in a spiritual reality, in incorporeal, spiritual beings—God being the supreme spiritual being. The second sense of the term involves a feeling of connectedness to something grander, larger, more encompassing than the self, in which the self is embedded. It is a heightened emotional, naturalistic, and psychological experience. It can be a sense of being connected to the universe, the earth, nature, the human race, living creatures, the arts, etc. I think it valid to say that all those interviewed saw themselves as being spiritual in at least one, and sometimes both, definitions of the term. All sought to live lives that held purpose and meaning.

Paths to Creativity

In reviewing the stories it was quite apparent that people took different routes to creativity. It also became evident that their creative and productive activities often bore some relationship to their age or life stage; that their interests and aspirations from earlier stages in life frequently were applied in new ways in later life; and that creativity played a role in helping individuals cope with loss and adversity.

Different Routes

As we have seen in the narratives, the paths or routes individuals took to their creative activities varied greatly. They ranged from the continuation of careers, to the application of work or career skills in new ways and in new settings, to the further development of avocations, and to brand new endeavors. The number of individuals in chapters three and four and five was considerably greater than the number in chapter two, indicating that with this particular collection of individuals, many more sought activities that were not work or career related.

Activities could be divided broadly into service activities and artistic activities, with some individuals combining both. In addition, a few people were involved in athletic pursuits and others in scholarly/academic endeavors.

Pre-retirement planning differed among those interviewed. Some knew exactly what they wanted to do and already had activities or plans in place prior to retirement. Others had tentative plans and still others had no plans at all. It is possible that, after a demanding work life, some in this latter group needed a period of rest and rehabilitation before contemplating, and expending energy on, a new enterprise.

As noted earlier, people had different energy levels and the amount of time and effort they devoted to their creative activities varied. Some were extremely busy all day, every day, and that worked well for them. Others carefully paced themselves in accordance with their levels of energy and stamina.

These different routes and styles show us that there is no one particular "right way." Different paths work for different people.

Creativity Related to Age and Life Stage

At the time they were interviewed, the participants in this book ranged in age from sixty to ninety-five. There are obvious and significant differences within such a large age spread.

In the process of looking back at the ages or life stages when many participants began their creative careers, some patterns or relationships became apparent. Two examples from the narratives illustrating the relationship of life stage and the development of creative activities follow.

————————

The process that eventually led to my commitment (to conservation) goes back to my midlife crisis. I married when I got out of school, which is what one did. I raised two splendid children and when they grew up I asked myself "what now?" I could become a proper matron, I could become a first-class alcoholic or I could do something else. I chose the latter path. I was almost fifty years old and had never been away from home by myself.

Shirley Caldwell Patterson

Shirley's search for purpose in her life and her passage to independence led her to Greek archeology, and then to backpacking and fly-fishing in the Wyoming wilderness, which in turn led to decades of groundbreaking work in the field of conservation. The popular and familiar term, "midlife crisis" used by Shirley to describe this turning point in her life, is seen by those who write about human development as a period or stage of reevaluation and quest. Often experienced by people in their forties and fifties, it is a time of searching to make life and work more meaningful and gratifying. The start of new avocations in midlife, which we saw in some of the narratives, can also be seen in this context.

————————

My interest in art and photography dates back to my early school days when I spent a lot of time visiting galleries and museums. I graduated from high school during the Depression and had to go to work and couldn't go to college. Four years before retiring, I started taking art and photography courses at night. I had felt deprived of learning all my life so I tried to catch up.

John Chan

John went on to fulfill his long-held aspirations, received a college degree at age seventy-six and became a very accomplished, internationally known photographer. John's story exemplifies what Gene D. Cohen in his book, *The Creative Age: Awakening Human Potential in the Second Half of Life*,[4] identifies as a Liberation Phase. Most apparent in people in their sixties and early seventies, it is characterized by a sense of freedom that comes with retirement and the readiness on the part of individuals to break out of conventions and routines. It is the time when the feeling of "if not now, when?" is translated into actions. Many of those interviewed experienced this sense of liberation and the desire to break from the usual and go in new directions prior to, or following, retirement.

Age or life stage also played some role in the types and combinations of activities in which people were involved. A number of individuals, such as Laurie Naiman, Marilynn Rosenthal, Bill Valenzuela and Henry Foster, all in their seventies, had overlapping careers and still maintained some involvement in their pre-retirement careers or jobs at the same time they pursued their newer or expanding creative endeavors. They worked on a limited or part-time basis, taught a course or two, consulted, or went on medical rounds, concurrent with their creative activities.

Others had sequential creative careers, and segued from one to another, as they grew older. For instance, in her sixties Molly Agras slowly decreased the time and energy that she put into her interior design business, and in her seventies she began to devote more time to fundraising for a homeless shelter. Helen Hill made a transition over time from full-time advocacy for the mentally ill, which she had done in her sixties and seventies, to teaching older adults how to write memoirs when in her eighties. These latter careers tended to be less demanding than the earlier ones. A small number of individuals were employed in brand new second careers. For example, Don Majors, age sixty, retired early and went from employment as a pipe fitter to working as an assistant to a U.S. congressman. Age was a relevant factor in these overlapping, sequential and new careers.

One creative activity, that was more in evidence among the older interviewees, was memoir and autobiographical writing. These forms of writing, along with storytelling, are all forms of life review; they are ways to affirm identity, to look at the influences, choices and accomplishments in one's life and gain perspective. Writing memoirs and storytelling are also means of educating younger people about history and younger family members about their roots. Here is one example from the stories:

After a couple of years [of leading the memoir writing group] someone in the group said, "What's fair is fair. It's time for you to write something." I joined the group as a writer then and have enjoyed mining my own life since. I think the writing [memoirs] has meant a lot to all of us. You remember things you hadn't thought of for a long time and writing about them gives you perspective and understanding.

Helen Hill

A sense of urgency or pressure, to do as much as possible before it was too late, was expressed by many but was more apparent in those of advanced age. Fay Kleinman, at age ninety-four, expressed it in the following way:

Why am I getting more and more ideas now for paintings (and writing) than I've ever had before? I'd like to know the answer to that. Is it because time is short and I instinctively know that, so something is moving faster in me?

Continuity from Earlier Stages in Life

Continuity was evident as individuals brought their experiences, values, commitments, skills and aspirations from the past and applied them in new ways in the present. The connection to the past was obvious when individuals continued to use their career skills in some fashion or pursued their established avocations. It was also apparent when long-held aspirations were consciously planned for, and realized.

Of interest is the fact that even those who had no plans for retirement ended up rediscovering and/or combining past interests, talents, aspirations and the things they had loved to do. For instance, Lois Kivi Nochman had no retirement plans and didn't start swimming competitively until five years after retirement. Yet, when one looks at her background, swimming was an important aspect of her early life and competitive swimming, which she would have loved, had not been available to girls and women in high school and college. She has now made up for that in spades!

Joy Scott, who describes herself as a late bloomer, responded to a newspaper article, which mentioned that the local UNA shop needed volunteers. At the time, she was sixty-eight years old and did not have a clear retirement plan. She eventually became one of the managers and buyers for the shop. Her present position draws on and combines past aspects of her life. It satisfies her deep and long-standing commitment to the ideals of the United Nations and to UNICEF; she had been an active fundraiser for UNICEF when her children were young. It also enables her to use her previously acquired knowledge and love of ethnic arts and crafts.

Lois Schwartz, as a result of being invited to a dinner designed to find donors for the University of Michigan's School of Music, created a new and original role for herself as a support person for recent graduates embarking on performance careers in New York City. In this role, she has combined a unique blend of long-standing interests and talents—extensive knowledge and love of music, networking skills, familiarity with the New York City music scene, fondness for her alma mater and a desire to help and nurture young people.

Creativity Growing Out of Loss and Adversity

Loss is an inevitable part of life as people age, and almost everyone among this group of thirty-seven had experienced the painful and profound loss of partners, children, siblings or dear friends. Many handled their losses by developing new relationships or investing more in the ones they already had. In addition to loss, a number of individuals had experienced considerable trauma and/or adversity in the course of their lives. These painful experiences fueled their creativity; and their creative activities, in turn, helped them cope with their experiences of loss and trauma.

Carrie Lo speaks of turning to watercolor painting to ease her grief following her husband's death. It helped her get through that very difficult time and she continues to see painting as a therapeutic outlet as well as a source of joy.

Jai-Zhen Song, a composer and conductor, dealt with the trauma of a life-threatening illness through his music. He believes that channeling his emotions of pain, fear and loneliness into his composing kept him alive.

Miriam Brysk, a Holocaust survivor, experienced a resurgence of feelings and memories after a visit to the ghettos and concentration camps of Eastern Europe. This led her to develop her unique and powerful art. In her artwork, she honors those murdered and tells their stories, hoping to ensure they are not lost to history. Miriam also wrote an autobiography, entitled *Shattered Childhood*, which is about her Holocaust experience and her difficult early years in the United States.

Barbara Jones turned adversity into an opportunity. Her daughter, who had an addiction problem, gave birth to a child at age sixteen. Barbara assumed responsibility for raising her granddaughter and saw it as her "second chance." She later used her experience to educate social work professionals about the needs of family caregivers. Her role contributed to grandparents, and other care-giving relatives, receiving sensitive and appropriate assistance.

Others who coped with their grief in creative ways include Marilynn Rosenthal and Shirley Caldwell-Patterson. Marilynn researched and wrote a book about 9/11, in an effort to understand the horrible tragedy that caused her son's death. Shirley compiled, co-edited and published a book of a dear friend's writings. Both of them created learning centers or lecture series, which benefit and educate others, while honoring the memory of those they lost.

How Did They Do It?   What Did It Take?

I've had to cope with a lot of things in my life—losses, disappointments, and struggles. But now I have a great life and my children have good lives. And I love what I am doing.

Albine Bech

How did these thirty-seven older individuals go about pursuing the endeavors that were so meaningful to them, and for which they felt passion and commitment? Beyond the preconditions they all shared, what did it take? In looking over the stories, consistent characteristics and behaviors emerge. No one had all the characteristics and behaviors but everyone displayed a combination of some of them.

Challenging Negative Stereotypes

No one accepted the negative stereotypes of aging, which are still present in our society. Individuals were optimistic; they displayed confidence in their competence and abilities and didn't believe the stereotypes applied to them. In conjunction with this, they didn't accept the norms from an earlier generation of how older people should act. This sometimes meant challenging the norms they had internalized, as well as not acquiescing, or conforming to, certain social conventions held by others of how they should "act their age." For example, people questioned Bill Valenzuela's continuing community involvement saying, "Why are you doing all of this at your age? Are you crazy? You should be taking it easy or out playing golf." He was able to withstand the social pressure and his response has been that he is doing what he wants to do, he feels it is where he belongs, and his work in the community still helps others.

Self-reflection

For some individuals, the years preceding and following retirement were a time for reflection. Their awareness of their mortality and the passage of time prompted thoughts about how they wanted to live the rest of their lives. In this inward looking process, individuals contemplated and reevaluated their priorities and beliefs, and what they saw as the sources of gratification and meaning. Priorities and beliefs had often shifted from an earlier time in life. This introspection played a role in motivating and spurring them into action.

There was great variation in the amount of time individuals spent on this type of reflection, as well as the amount of conscious awareness they had regarding the process itself. Some report not being aware of doing any of it, but nonetheless, they had reached a state of knowing how they wanted to live and what was important to them at their stage in life. For some, self-reflection occurred after they had followed up on an opportunity and realized the gratification and meaning it provided them. The changes they had already made led them to more conscious reflection.

In some cases, a change in life circumstances after retirement led to a reevaluation of priorities. Frank Nibley, for instance, says that his plans and priorities changed after being diagnosed and treated for a life-threatening cancer. He recognized he had enjoyed a great life and now wanted to give something back.

Visualization

For many, the process of actually visualizing, or having a mental image of themselves in a certain role or activity, gave it an added sense of reality and possibility. This was the case with Carrie Raiford. She had dreamed of being a public speaker and could see herself performing in front of an audience. This contributed to the ease with which she accepted and embraced the role of storyteller once it was offered to her.

Accepting, Seeing and Creating Opportunities

Opportunities, some more serendipitous than others, played an important role in many of the stories. In their retirement, Robert Kahn, Henry Foster and Carleen McGinn were offered opportunities based on their professional competencies and reputations. They had not sought positions with the MacArthur Foundation, Pathfinder International or Stephen Ministry, respectively. Similarly, Lois Nochman and Albine Bech were presented opportunities based on their abilities. They, too, had not initially sought them. For others, it was a matter of seeing something, or being somewhere, at the right time and place. Everyone was open to opportunities, they did not shy away, they took advantage of them, and as a result, they thrived.

Others were more proactive and saw a situation or event, or series of events, as an opportunity to form organizations or create special roles for themselves. This was the case with Shirley Caldwell Patterson, who helped found the Cumberland River Compact, and Lois Schwartz, who created her "Auntie Mame" role.

Risk-Taking and Experimentation

The new ventures and opportunities people pursued brought with them a sense of risk. The status quo, even when it is a less preferable option, feels comfortable and familiar; change has an unknown element and requires some courage. Objectively, some risks were greater than others, such as the Campbells' move to a decaying area in hopes of bringing about neighborhood renewal. But everyone who moved in a new direction, or experimented with one, felt some anxiety or apprehension. For instance, enrolling in a college program, as Amatullah Saleem did, can raise fears of failure, concerns about one's sense of competence and whether one can measure up to the other students, particularly the younger students.

They were all able to tolerate, or live with, their fears and apprehensions and did not let these feelings deter them from their objectives. When apprehensive about taking next steps, some turned to others who could offer them support and encouragement about moving forward.

There was a counterbalance to the sense of risk and the accompanying feelings of apprehension and anxiety. At this stage in life, people tended to have fewer work and family responsibilities, so they had less to lose in experimenting and trying new activities. Their past successes and their life experiences also provided them with self-confidence and perspective.

Planning and Implementing

Individuals pursued activities that were realistic and doable. They recognized their own limitations, particularly their physical limitations, and didn't go after unreachable, unrealistic objectives.

The amount of planning we saw in the narratives varied. David Herzig provides an example of someone who charted and followed through on a concrete course of action. Prior to retiring, he made plans to take courses and acquire skills in woodworking. The first course he took after retirement was followed by further courses, which eventually led him to construct a woodworking shop in his basement. He then proceeded to challenge himself with different and increasingly more difficult projects. David had taken concrete action steps, each building on the other. This step-by-step approach leading to a goal was helpful to many people. It made the tasks feel manageable and the completion of each step led to a greater sense of mastery and confidence.

Working Hard, Persevering, and Acquiring Competence

Individuals worked hard at acquiring competence. They took classes or taught themselves skills; they educated themselves and kept themselves informed on issues; they practiced, experimented and devoted time and energy to their endeavors. They persevered despite setbacks they experienced in reaching their goals. For example, Dean Bush, who taught himself how to make and repair musical instruments, initially did not have good results with his violin making. In response, he intensified his research and became more knowledgeable about the construction of, and preferred woods for, the violin. With experimentation, practice and experience, his violins improved.

Success Furthered Success

Mastery of endeavors brought about increased self-confidence and a sense of purpose. It often contributed to feelings of excitement and was energizing. The internal satisfaction experienced by individuals was more important to them than recognition they might receive from others. This internal satisfaction or sense of success reinforced the motivation to continue and sometimes expand activities. Marvin Nochman, the actor, added directing to his theater work. Joy Scott assumed more responsibilities at the UNA shop and Berdelle Taylor Campbell increased the amount and range of her community involvement.

I still get emotional highs with every production. There is so much ego satisfaction. I'm thinking, "This is my scene, I can do it, I'm going to make you enjoy it." I'm eighty-four years old and it is a pleasure to work with younger people: it energizes me.
                                                                    Marvin Nochman

My responsibilities at the shop have grown over the years. Initially I didn't plan to be as involved as I am now. I now put in a considerable amount of time each week and it is where my heart is, in supporting the UNA and the United Nations. I can't think of any other volunteer activity that would pull on my heartstrings like this one.
                                                                    Joy Scott

Everything I do in the community relates to everything else I do. I believe that if a person can contribute, he or she jolly well should. But I'm not doing it because I should. I'd be denying myself if I didn't contribute as I get so much satisfaction out of what I do. I love this time in my life. I've never had so much fun.
                                                                    Berdelle Taylor Campbell

Questions and Suggestions for the Reader's Reflection

Take some time and try to visualize your retirement years. You may already be there, or it may be two, five, ten, even fifteen years from now. Where do you see yourself? What would you like to be doing?

Based on what we have learned, the questions and suggestions that follow may serve as starting points to help you think about your future.

The maintenance of cognitive and physical functioning, along with strong social and emotional connections, played a role in the overall well-being of those interviewed, and provided them with the foundation or support for creative and productive endeavors. The first three questions address those issues.

1. Looking ahead, are there relationships you want to improve and nurture, as well as social connections you would like to expand?
2. What activities might you build into your life as you grow older to help ensure maintenance of high cognitive functioning?
3. What do you need to do to maintain or improve your physical functioning and fitness? What type of regular physical exercise can you incorporate into your life?
4. Are there spiritual or religious pathways you would like to pursue?
5. Do the negative stereotypes of aging, or the norms from previous generations of how to "act your age" still influence or have power over you? Do you need to counteract them in your own thinking? Are there people you can turn to for support when dealing with restrictive social pressures?

6. The individuals interviewed all felt passion and commitment for the things they were doing. Their activities held meaning and importance for them and added excitement to their lives. Are there activities that you would like to continue that currently provide you with such feelings of purpose and pleasure? Are there endeavors that are not part of your life but you think might give you such feelings and are worth looking into and trying out?

7. People took different paths or routes to their creative activities. It would be useful to think about the paths that would best suit you. Do you want to continue doing something you are already doing? Would you like to do something different but use the skills you already have? Would you like to pursue something new?

8. If you are interested in a new direction, but are uncertain what, you might keep in mind that many of those who started new ventures did something that had relevance, or a connection, to earlier periods in their lives. Was there something you loved to do in the past that you would like to return to? Are there unrealized dreams, talents, or interests that you have never been able to act on, but would like to experiment with now, or in the near future?

9. Would you prefer doing something involving community service or the arts? Or would you like to combine the two?

10. If you were to bring effort and commitment to them, are the plans you are considering realistic and doable? Are they a good match for your physical level of functioning and your energy level and stamina?

11. Once you have some tentative ideas or plans, keep in mind that it is normal to experience some feelings of anxiety, or even fear, when you start taking steps towards your objectives. Managing those feelings so that they don't prevent you from

proceeding is important. At those times it can be helpful to do some "self-talk"—think about your past accomplishments as well as how you successfully coped with other challenges and transitions. And consider, what do you really lose in trying? Also, don't forget that you can experiment with different things until you find what feels like a good fit for you. Relaxation techniques, as well as turning to others for support and encouragement, can also be helpful when experiencing anxiety prior to starting something new.

12. Many found that a one-step-at-a-time approach was useful and made objectives manageable when launching on a new course of action. A first step might be getting a catalogue from a community college or finding out when and where an organization holds meetings. Are there any first steps you can think of taking?

References and Notes

Chapter 1
In Search of Role Models

1. Cohen, G.D. *The Creative Age: Awakening Human Potential in the Second Half of Life.* New York: HarperCollins, 2000.

2. Freedman, M. *Prime Time: How Baby Boomers Will Revolutionize Retirement and Transform America.* New York: Public Affairs, 1999.

3. Rowe, J.W., and R.L. Kahn. *Successful Aging.* New York: Pantheon, 1998.

4. U.S. Bureau of the Census (2006). 65+ in the United States: 2005. Washington, D.C. Government Printing Office.

5. _____ "Census Report Foresees No Crisis Over Aging Generation's Health." New York *Times*, March 10, 2006.

6. Relin, D.O. "Don't Call Them Old, Call Them..." *Parade*, March 19, 2006.

7. Sadler, W.A. *The Third Age.* De Capo Press, 2000.

8. _____ "Dramatic Changes in U.S. Aging Highlighted in New Census." NIH Report." March 9, 2006   News Release-National Institutes of Health (NIH).

9. Riley, M.W., and Riley, J.W. "Structural Lag, Past and Future." In Riley, M.W., et al., eds., *Age and Structural Lag.* New York: John Wiley, 1994.

10. Kolata, G. "Old but Not Frail: A Matter of Heart and Head." New York *Times*, October 5, 2006. The article reports on rigorous studies by Dr. Becca Levy, a psychologist at Yale University and Dr. Thomas Hess, a psychologist at North Carolina State University. Dr. Levy is quoted as saying that some people may have difficulty resisting the pervasive negative stereotypes, accept them without realizing it, and they then become self-fulfilling prophecies.

11. Cohen, G.D. *The Creative Age: Awakening Human Potential in the Second Half of Life.* New York: HarperCollins, 2000.
Dr. Cohen's three categories include creativity that commences with age,

creativity that continues, sometimes changing, and creativity that connects with loss.

Chapter 2
Creativity Continuing and Work Skills Applied in New Ways

1. All interviews were tape-recorded and the narratives were condensed and edited by the author. Drafts were sent to the interviewees for their approval and changes were made when requested.
2. Rowe, J. W., and R. L. Kahn. *Successful Aging.* New York: Pantheon, 1998.

Chapter 4
Community Service—"Giving Back"

1. Erickson, E. *Childhood and Society.* New York: W.W. Norton, 1950.
2. Freedman, M. *Prime Time: How Baby Boomers Will Revolutionize Retirement and Transform America.* New York: Public Affairs, 1999.
3. Freedman, M. *Encore: Finding Work That Matters in the Second Half of Life.* New York: Public Affairs, 2007.

Chapter 5
Community-Based Art and Service Programs for Older Citizens

1. The Creativity and Aging Study: The Impact of Professionally Conducted Cultural Programs on Older Adults. Preliminary Results, March 10, 2005. Study Sponsored by the National Endowment for the Arts and George Washington University.
   Initial findings of this study found that regular involvement in participatory art programs had health promotion and disease prevention effects. Participants reported fewer doctors' visits; they had less need for medication and were less prone to depression than the control group.
2. Brown, P.L. "Retirees Discover a Place to Foster Their Inner Artist." New York *Times,* September 10, 2006.
3. Fried, L.P., Carson, M.C., Freedman, M., et al., "A Social Model for Health Promotion for an Aging Population: Initial Evidence on the

Experience Corps Model," *Journal of Urban Health* 81(1), March 2004. The authors of the study indicated that participation in the Experience Corps had the potential to increase the physical, mental and social activity of the participants, all of which are linked to better health in later life.

Chapter 6
Living Longer and Better

1. Rowe, J.W., and R.L. Kahn. *Successful Aging*. New York: Pantheon, 1998
2. U.S. Department of Health and Human Services (1996). Physical Activity and Health. A report by the Surgeon General. Atlanta, Georgia: U.S. Department of Health and Human Services, Centers for Disease Control and Prevention, National Center for Chronic Disease Prevention and Health Promotion.

   The positive role of regular exercise is confirmed in the 1996 Surgeon General's Report. The report, which draws on a large number of studies, finds that regular physical exercise not only benefits mental and physical functioning, it also reduces the risk of many diseases, and helps to preserve the independence of older adults.
3. Phone conversation held in September 2006.
4. Cohen, G. D. *The Creative Age: Awakening Human Potential in the Second Half of Life*. HaperCollins, New York: 2000.

Other References

Butler, R.N. (1963) The Life Review: An Interpretation of Reminiscence in the Aged. *Psychiatry* 26, 65-76.

Butler R.N. (1997) Living Longer, Contributing Longer. *JAMA,* Vol. 278, No.16.

Friedan, B. *The Fountain of Age*. New York: Touchstone, 1994.

Goldman, G., and Mahler, R. *Secrets of Becoming a Late Bloomer*. Center City, MN: Hazelden, 1995.

Higgins, C. *Elder Grace*. New York: Bulfinch Press, 2000.

Levenson, D.J. *The Seasons of a Man's Life*. New York: Knopf, 1978.

Tenneson, J. *Wise Women*. New York: Bulfinch Press, 2002.

Tenneson, J. *Amazing Men*. New York: Bulfinch Press, 2004.

Vaillant, G.E. *Aging Well*. New York: Little Brown and Company, 2002.

List of Contributors

Acknowledgements

This book would not have been possible without the assistance and participation of many people. First, and above all, I want to thank three of them: my good friend and colleague, Penny Tropman, my daughter, Ann, and my husband, Mayer. All three gave me support and encouragement, and their shared belief in the value of this project sustained me. They generously took time from their busy schedules to read drafts of the manuscript and offered invaluable advice. I am also grateful to Joanne Brownstein of Brandt and Hochman Literary Agents for her editorial suggestions and for prodding me to share more of myself in the book.

A number of friends and acquaintances whom I think of as my "scouts," in addition to professionals in agencies serving older clientele, helped me locate and paved the way for me to meet the people whose stories are presented in the book. In New York City, my thanks to my scout Lois Schwartz, and to Barbara Berkman and Ada Mui, both of Columbia University School of Social Work, to Susan Perlstein at the National Center for Creative Aging, Marsha Gilden at Elders Share the Arts, and Isabel Ching, Director of the City Hall Senior Citizen Center. My invaluable scouts in Nashville, Tennessee, included Berdelle Campbell, Susan Bell, Mary Early-Zald and Deana Claiborne. In Tucson, Arizona, Carolyn Sanger was of great help, as was Lynda Krause at the Volunteer Center of Southern Arizona. In Ann Arbor, Michigan, both Ruth Campbell, at the University of Michigan's Turner Resource Center, and Phyllis Herzig, at the Washtenaw County Jewish Community Center, generously assisted me in locating and contacting interviewees. My thanks to Helen Hasenfeld, Zeke Hasenfeld and Joy Scott in California, as well as Tim Carpenter, Director of More than Shelter for Seniors, and Bill Watanabe, Director of the Little Tokyo Service Center. I am indebted to all of them.

I also want to express my appreciation to the following people whom I interviewed, but whose stories I could not include because of space constraints: Wenyu Li in New York City; Letitia Byrd and Gavin Williams in Southeastern Michigan; Mary Granholm, Henry Kushlan, Genevieve Oxley and Edie Kirshner, all from the San Francisco Bay Area. I learned much from all of them and regret I was not able to include their interesting and informative stories.

And, of course, my enduring gratitude to all those whose stories made this book possible. I began this search for creative and productive older individuals due to my own apprehension about what lay ahead as I grew older. The search gave me the opportunity to meet and get to know some wonderful people. I feel fortunate and honored that they were all willing to share their stories with me. Despite some limitations and some profound personal losses, their lives are filled with purpose, meaning, growth, satisfaction and joy. Drawing on a lifetime of experience and knowledge, they have contributed in significant ways to their families, communities and beyond. I could not have asked for better role models.